D0207516

AHEAD OF
THEIR TIME

AHEAD OF THEIR TIME

A Biographical Dictionary of Risk-Taking Women

Joyce Duncan

GREENWOOD PRESS
Westport, Connecticut • London

Library of Congress Cataloging-in-Publication Data

Duncan, Joyce, 1946–
    Ahead of their time : a biographical dictionary of risk-taking women / Joyce Duncan.
        p. cm.
    Includes bibliographical references and index.
    ISBN 0–313–31660–0 (alk. paper)
    1. Women—Biography—Dictionaries. I. Title.
    HQ1123.D86 2002
    920.72—dc21   2001038357

British Library Cataloguing in Publication Data is available.

Library of Congress Catalog Card Number: 2001038357
ISBN: 0–313–31660–0

First published in 2002

Greenwood Press, 88 Post Road West, Westport, CT 06881
An imprint of Greenwood Publishing Group, Inc.
www.greenwood.com

Printed in the United States of America

The paper used in this book complies with the
Permanent Paper Standard issued by the National
Information Standards Organization (Z39.48–1984).

10 9 8 7 6 5 4 3 2 1

Contents

Introduction

Lady an explorer? a traveller in skirts?
The notion's just a trifle too seraphic:
Let them stay and mind the babies, or hem our ragged shirts;
But they mustn't, can't and shan't be geographic.
                                        —*Punch Magazine*, 1893

When I first undertook this study, I had some knowledge of the women throughout history who merited inclusion in such a work, but I had no idea of how many had broken traditional bounds and ventured into unchartered territory. As the months of digging for facts proceeded, I was amazed, often overwhelmed, and thoroughly fascinated by what I unearthed. As an instructor of literature, I often preach to students about the lack of possibilities that were open to women during certain periods, but all the while Kate Chopin's Mrs. Mallard and Ibsen's Nora and other fictional characters, often created by men, were bemoaning their prescribed existence, tied to their husbands and subjected to their wills, real women like Mary Kingsley and Isabella Bishop were tramping through the jungles of Africa, sailors like Isabelle Autissier and Clare Francis were fighting squalls and drifting around the world in small craft, fliers like Amelia Earhart and Harriet Quimby were soaring solo through the skies, anthropologists and archaeologists like Margaret Mead and Ruth Benedict were preserving history in order to learn from it, and environmentalists and naturalists like Anne LaBastille and Rachel Carson were fighting to preserve the habitats of the world for future generations. Together they constructed the groundwork for distaff polar explorers, deep-sea divers, and astronauts to come.

As my work progressed, I often became so involved in the reading and the domino theory of research that I would forget to make notes and nearly forgot, as the deadline neared, that it was my assignment to process the material and create something new of it. At last faced with the possibility of missing that deadline, I was forced to begin writing, leaving further study for a future date. Even in the writing process, however, I found myself "becoming" these intrepid, intractable women as they lived with gorillas, plunged into the Arctic, played nosy with sharks, and rocketed into space. As I sat in the comfort zone of my writing desk, I was struck with awe, envy, and intense wanderlust, living vicariously through women whose lives were more intriguing than any character gracing the pages of literature anthologies. They took on mythical proportion and often it was difficult to separate the *mythos* from the *logos*, to disinter the truth buried under the mythology. In the case of the earlier women, there were often multiple sources of information that were frequently contradictory; for the more modern adventurers, history often changed as the research progressed; in fact, the Bancroft expedition was not completed until only a few hours before the manuscript was.

I must admit to being one of those peculiar academic types who actually enjoys research. I often tell college freshmen who are beginning the process to look at research as a video game—one has to crawl through tunnels and knock down walls to rescue the princess. As I stumbled through libraries, collections of biographies, archives, periodicals, and Web sites, my initial list of entries expanded. I was occasionally diverted by a particular female scoundrel among the lot, but slowly the group divided into those who had journeyed by land, by sea, and by air. It also became obvious that these adventurers were not alone; there was a trend among women that began, in earnest, in the late 1700s and continues to the present day. In an attempt to show this continuity, I considered it imperative to juxtapose the earlier explorers with their modern counterparts.

To that end, I ventured back to the Victorian lady travelers in their camel- and donkey-driven peregrinations across Africa, Asia, and South America and forward to current and often treacherous treks across the frozen wastelands of Antarctica; from the earliest efforts in aviation, where a record flight covered only a few hundred miles, to twentieth-century astronauts conquering the edges of the universe; from the earliest interest in water navigation by Mary Kingsley, to the women of today who circumnavigate the globe alone in sailing vessels; and from Beatrice Grimshaw's initial diving ventures in 1909 off the coast of New

Guinea, to Eugenie Clark's dynamic research in the depths of the Red Sea.

Although I discovered a great many more collections of biographies of women explorers than I expected, I did not find any that were as inclusive as I try to be here. Works were available on mountaineers, explorers, and aviators but none incorporated all three categories, and almost all excluded the more recent updates in each category. None included lesser known but equally important anthropologists, archaeologists, environmentalists, naturalists, sailors, or adventurers.

One would have expected most of the women researched for this project to have little in common because of their diverse social backgrounds and the century that often separated them, yet throughout the project I was struck by a growing list of similarities among them. Most considered what they were doing as "work," whether they were compensated or not. Many of them had troubled relationships with their parents, particularly their fathers, by whom they were either ostracized or overly attached, and the majority were involved in multiple relationships with men, often marrying several times or not at all. They were either largely self-taught or highly educated, often holding degrees in English. Many were educators as well as explorers, and almost all were photographers, environmentalists, and horsewomen. Most were activists in a cross section of causes from multiculturalism to women's rights, from protecting ecosystems to protecting vanishing civilizations. Each, it seemed, wrote prolifically and successfully. Together, they redefined what it means to be a woman and turned their world into a planet without borders. The overwhelming commonality was one of the spirit—they were willing to go where others fear to tread, willingly, almost compulsively, to undertake the unknown—simply because it was there.

Women selected for inclusion in this work displayed the shared characteristics of going beyond what was expected, either by their era or their gender or both. Others of the same fortitude were considered but rejected either because they were outside the determined parameters of air, sea, and land or because they could scarcely be considered role models. The women identified in the vignettes are in that category, not because they should be admired less but only because less information about their lives was available. The work is organized alphabetically for ease of use. Each entry includes the years in which the woman lived, her nationality, and field of endeavor. An effort was made to include women from across the globe; however, more information was available on those from the United States and from England. That occurred because the study was done in the United States and should not be considered preferential. Each major entry includes a list of references and suggesting reading.

Any endeavor of this type cannot be taken alone. Thanks must be paid to my colleague and friend, Marcia Songer, who walked into my office and asked if I had time to write a book, and to my editor, Lynn Malloy, who graciously accepted my affirmative response to that question. She also displayed infinite patience as I waded through the process of putting the work together. My appreciation also to Mel Page, the editor of the listserv H-Africa, who discovered one piece of missing information I could find nowhere else; to the creators of the AskJeeves network, who almost always located the obscure data for fact checking; and to my cadre of friends, especially Teresa and Jamey, who kept the faith.

AHEAD OF
THEIR TIME

Harriet Chalmers Adams
(1875–1937)

United States
Explorer

Courtesy of the Library of Congress

By the time she helped found and was elected the first president of the Society of Women Geographers in 1925, Harriet Chalmers Adams was already a reputed amateur anthropologist and inveterate adventurer, having logged hundreds of thousands of miles during her travels. Called the foremost explorer of her time, she is perhaps best remembered for her exhaustive three-year trek through Central and South America.

Harriet Chalmers Adams was born in Stockton, California, in 1875. Her father, Alexander Chalmers, was an engineer from Scotland who had crossed the United States seeking adventure and perhaps gold near the Pacific. Her mother was Frances Wilkins, whose parents were early settlers in California. Instilling an initial love of travel and discovery in his child, Alexander Chalmers took his eight-year-old daughter on a horseback tour of the entire state, including extended visits to the Sierra Nevada Mountains. That trip molded the direction her life would take, and from then on, she expressed a desire to go to the "ends of the earth." Although she had no formal education after age eleven, Harriet gained a deep respect for learning from her parents and from private tutors.

In 1899 Harriet married M. Franklin Pierce Adams, an electrical engineer who shared her wanderlust. During their extended honeymoon in Mexico in 1900, Harriet was quite taken with the Spanish people whose friendliness to foreigners was unexpected, considering the negative stereotype attached to those of Spanish descent in the day. Upon returning to California she immediately began to plan a protracted stay south of the border in order to familiarize herself with the customs of the people with whom she had become so enamored.

In 1903 the Adamses departed for an extended excursion through Central and South America. Traveling on horseback, initially sidesaddle but eventually Western-style, Harriet and her husband scaled the Andes Mountains, explored ancient Incan ruins, stalked through the jungle, tangled with vampire bats, and slept on the ground under the stars. Over the three years of their journey, Harriet Adams logged over forty thousand miles and reached points previously unknown to any white woman. She was fascinated by the indigenous populations of the region and saddened by what had happened to their once glorious culture, often by conquest or through the intervention of well-intentioned missionaries.

At times Franklin Adams was called away by his new appointment to the Pan American Union, and Harriet continued, undeterred, by herself. In contrast to many of her generation, she felt her gender was not a handicap and that women should be able to experience life as fully as men. She visited the cities of South America and investigated the emerging role of women in that society, later publishing the information in *Ladies Home Journal* and other venues.

After returning to the United States Adams joined the lecture circuit, illustrating her presentations with the slides and photographs she had taken and attempting to dispel many of the myths that had led to prejudice against those of Spanish descent. She was immediately in demand, although many failed to believe a woman capable of such feats. Through her lectures she raised enough money between 1906 and 1908 to finance her next expedition. While touring South America Adams had become convinced that travelers from Asian countries were the first to settle the Americas and that the native Indian populations were descended from Asian stock. Her next jaunt was designed to prove that theory.

In 1910 she crossed Haiti on horseback and over the next few years traveled through the Philippines and from Siberia to Sumatra. In all she visited every Latin American country and every nation that had a Spanish or Portuguese connection. From the Caribbean to the Far East, she studied ancient peoples who could have been allied with the earliest American population. Although she may not have definitively proved her thesis, after each foray she returned to many lecture engagements and publishing demands, including being a frequent contributor to *National Geographic*.

During World War I Harriet Adams, not being one to sit quietly by and roll bandages, contacted *Harper's Magazine* and was assigned to the European theater. In 1916 she was one of the first correspondents at the French front and likely the only woman reporter to literally enter the trenches during that time.

Returning to her peripatetic pursuits after the war ended, Adams toured the regions of the Mediterranean. On a visit to the Balearic Islands, a province of eastern Spain, she tumbled from a sea wall and had to be rescued by passing fishermen. Doctors told her that, as a result of the broken back she incurred in the accident, she would likely be paralyzed and never walk again. Not having ever done the expected, Harriet, however, refused to succumb to a life without intrigue and after a few recuperative years, she was off again, visiting Spain, Northern Africa, and Asia Minor.

By 1933 Franklin had retired, and the Adamses opted for a more sedentary lifestyle, living in various European cities. Harriet Adams died peacefully in Nice, France, in 1937.

She was a member of various scientific and geographic associations, including the Royal Geographic Society (1913), and one of the four women founders of the Society of Women Geographers, to which she devoted over eight years, organizing the group and establishing the organization's headquarters in Washington, D.C. Though honored numerous times and regularly published due to her unconventional lifestyle, Harriet Chalmers Adams would likely prefer to be remembered as a humanitarian—one who not only cared about the indigenous peoples of the planet but also one who attempted to raise the consciousness of others on their behalf.

References and Suggested Reading

Adams, Harriet Chalmers. Articles in various issues of *National Geographic* from 1905 to 1937.

Adelman, Joseph. *Famous Women.* New York: Ellis Lonow Company, 1926.

Anema, Durlynn. *Harriet Chalmers Adams: Adventurer and Explorer.* New York: Morgan Reynolds, 1997.

James, Edward T., Janet W. James, and Paul S. Boyer, eds. *Notable American Women, 1607–1950.* Cambridge, MA: Harvard University Press, 1971.

Joy Friederike Victoria Gessner Adamson (1910–1980)

Austria
Conservationist

A conservationist and painter, Joy Adamson spent most of her adult life in Africa. Discouraged by the vanishing species of wildlife and the cultural assimilation of native peoples, Adamson devoted her life to memorializing on canvas the flora, fauna, and tribal customs of the Dark Continent. She rose to international fame with the book *Born Free* (1960), which chronicled her experiences with Elsa, a lion cub that she raised and returned to the wild. The work spawned a feature film, a hit song, and a television series.

Joy Friederike Victoria Gessner Adamson was born in Troppau, Silesia, a section of Austria-Hungary, and raised in Vienna. Her father, Victor, and mother, Traute, were divorced when Joy was ten years old. A prominent architect, Victor Gessner raised his daughter on a spacious estate replete with wildlife, and the young girl spent many hours accompanying the game warden on his rounds. Joy was educated in Vienna but appeared to have no early indication of where her talents lay. She studied piano but was not proficient enough to have a career as a classical pianist; she dabbled in dressmaking, bookbinding, and drawing and developed an interest in archaeology. She trained for a medical career but did not pass the entrance examinations to qualify for university courses.

In 1935 Joy Gessner married Victor von Klarwill, an Austrian who unwittingly guided her to what would become her destiny. On holiday with her husband in Kenya in 1937, she fell in love with the region as well as with Swiss botanist Peter Bally. After obtaining a divorce from Klarwill, Joy married Bally in 1938 and moved permanently to Africa. Theirs was an idyllic existence at first. Most of the time was spent out of doors in the Serengeti National Park or on safari. As Bally ventured into the wilds as part of his profession, Joy accompanied him, paint box in hand, and illustrated over seven hundred studies of flowers and trees native to Africa. Their perfect existence, however, was evidently doomed to failure, and Joy and Peter Bally were estranged, then divorced.

In 1944 Joy Gessner Klarwill Bally married George Adamson, an India-born British game warden who had worked in Kenya since 1924 as a gold prospector, a goat trader, and safari hunter. He was assigned to the North Frontier District, and over the next ten years Joy Adamson catalogued plant life in that region by illustrating seven books on African wild flowers and creating more than four thousand paintings, six hundred of which hang in the National Museum of Kenya. During the period she was also commissioned by the colonial government of Kenya to preserve, in portraiture, members of twenty-two tribes whose cultures were fading. The collection was published by Harcourt in 1967 as *The Peoples of Kenya*.

In 1956 George was attacked by a lioness, which he killed in self-defense, leaving behind a motherless cub. The Adamsons took the tiny feline into their home and hearts, raising it as a cross between a house cat and a child of their own. Previously the couple had developed Meru National Park as an animal refuge and eventually decided the cub, named Elsa, needed to be returned there to its native habitat. In order to survive in the open veldt of Meru National Park, Elsa had to be re-trained to hunt and to kill for food and protection. The job of acclimatization fell to Joy, who was criticized for her endeavor by some who felt Elsa's natural instinct would be to attack the species with which she was most familiar, which was, of course, human. Not easily dissuaded, however, Adamson deemed the grown cat ready, and Elsa was released into the park. The lioness not only survived but mated, often bringing her three cubs to visit her "foster family" in the encampment she had known as home.

Joy Adamson immortalized the time with Elsa in the trilogy *Born Free: A Lioness of Two Worlds* (1960), *Living Free: The Story of Elsa and Her Cubs* (1961), and *Forever Free: Elsa's Pride* (1962). Each of the three books climbed the best-seller list and was developed into a feature film. In 1966 the trilogy was condensed into one volume as *The Story of Elsa*. Joy Adamson continued returning animals to the wild, among them Pippa, a cheetah. Pippa's story is told in *The Spotted Sphinx*, published by Harcourt in 1969.

By the 1960s Joy Adamson was considered one of the world's leading conservationists. She founded the international funding group the Elsa Wild Animal Appeal in 1961 and helped launch the World Wildlife Fund in 1962. All proceeds from the books, films, and the song "Born Free" went into the Elsa Fund to finance conservation projects and educational endeavors.

The Adamsons separated in 1971, and Joy Adamson was found dead in northern Kenya in 1980. Initially, it was assumed that she had been mauled by a lion, but later a disgruntled employee was charged with her murder.

Joy Adamson almost singlehandedly promoted awareness of the need to protect Africa's wild animals from poachers, hunters, and collectors. In a *Washington Post* interview (August 10, 1970), she stated, "Man can rebuild a pyramid but he can't rebuild ecology or a giraffe." In addition to other honors she received the Royal Horticultural Society's Gold Grenfell Medal in 1947.

References and Suggested Reading

Adamson, Joy. *The Searching Spirit: An Autobiography*. New York: Harcourt, 1978.
Cass, Caroline. *Joy Adamson: Behind the Mask*. New York: Ulverscroft, 1994.

Neimark, Anne. *Wild Heart: The Story of Joy Adamson, Author of Born Free*. New York: Harcourt, Brace, 1999.
Publisher's Weekly (obituary). 18 January 1980, 42.
Uglow, Jennifer S. *The International Dictionary of Women's Biography*. New York: Continuum Press, 1982.
Variety (obituary). 16 January 1980, 52.

Elizabeth Cabot Cary
Agassiz
(1822–1907)

United States
Naturalist

E ducator, author, and naturalist, Elizabeth "Lizzie" Cary Agassiz was an astute observer and recorder of the natural world, as well as a pioneer in offering educational opportunities to women. With her husband, Swiss naturalist Jean Louis Agassiz, Elizabeth undertook several expeditions into South America and through the Straits of Magellan. After his death she founded an academic program for women, which eventually became Radcliffe College.

Elizabeth Cabot Cary Agassiz was born in Boston, Massachusetts, in 1822, the second of seven children. Her father was in the mercantile and financial world of the city, and little is known of her mother other than she was related to many of the city's prominent families. The young woman received no formal education but was tutored by her parents at home in topics such as art, music, and languages, which were considered appropriate to prepare her to assume her proper place in Boston society.

While attending a party hosted by her sister in 1846, Elizabeth met Jean Louis Agassiz, recently transplanted to the United States from Switzerland to accept the first professorship at Harvard University's new Lawrence Scientific School. In 1850, shortly after the death of his first wife, Agassiz married Elizabeth, even though she was sixteen years his junior, and overnight she became not only his wife but a stepmother to Louis's three children.

In 1855, partially to supplement the family income, Elizabeth Agassiz founded and operated a school for girls in her home in Cambridge. The school, which functioned for over eight years, was a pioneering effort in the almost nonexistent field of education for women, affording opportunities to many young girls who would not otherwise have had such an advantage.

In addition to taking copious notes on her husband's presentations, which subsequently were used as the text for the majority of his published works, Elizabeth organized and managed several of the couple's expeditions. The journey of greatest note was the two-year Thayer expedition to Brazil. Throughout the entire trip Louis obsessively collected fish of various families, while Elizabeth recorded everything she observed in her journal, including comments on an overnight stay at a "guest house" with many unattached young women, which she later discovered was actually a brothel. The expedition resulted in the publication of the co-written *A Journey in Brazil* (1867), which juxtaposed her personal observations of Brazilian culture with his lecture and field notes. Although some historians may view Elizabeth Agassiz as little more than a footnote to her husband's research, one reviewer pointed out that Elizabeth's journal reflections in the book contradict rather than support her husband's claims, especially those related to white superiority and the "otherness" of distinct cultures. Regardless of where the credit lies, the book became a best seller and a classic among natural historians.

From 1871 to 1872 the couple took two voyages on *The Hassler* through the Straits of Magellan, studying the effects of deep-sea dredging on the environment. After returning Elizabeth wrote and published articles in the *Atlantic Monthly*, which serve as the only account of discoveries regarding glaciation that Agassiz had noted during that excursion. Together they founded a school for the study of natural history on Penikese Island in Massachusetts and helped develop the Natural History Museum at Cambridge University. Between 1859 and 1865 Elizabeth Agassiz published several introductory guides to natural history and marine zoology, including *Actea: A First Lesson in Natural History* (1859) and *Seaside Studies in Natural History* (1865).

After Louis's death in 1873 Elizabeth penned a memoir of his life, *Louis Agassiz: His Life and Correspondence* (1885), while mulling over a plan to encourage the Harvard faculty to educate women at a separate facility. In 1879 this woman, who had received sparse and sporadic schooling herself, launched the Society for the Collegiate Instruction of Women in Cambridge, Massachusetts. In 1894 the institution's name was changed to Radcliffe College, and the facility became an official appendage of Harvard University. Elizabeth Agassiz served as the first president of the college, retaining that position until her retirement in 1899. She died as a result of a stroke in 1907.

Although she did not believe that men and women should be educated together, Elizabeth Agassiz was a strong advocate of a woman's right to learn. Perhaps it was her own loosely structured academic tutelage and her secondary role to her husband's discoveries that gave rise to her desire for women to receive an education equal to that of men.

References and Suggested Reading

Bergmann, Linda S. "A Troubled Marriage of Discourses." *Journal of American Culture* (Summer 1995): 83–89.

Paton, Lucy A. *Elizabeth Cary Agassiz: A Biography*. New York: Arno Press, 1974 (reprint).

Uglow, Jennifer S. *The International Dictionary of Women's Biography*. New York: Continuum, 1982.

Delia Denning Akeley
(1875–1970)

United States
Explorer

Courtesy of the Library of Congress

As the first Western woman to traverse the continent of Africa alone, from the Indian Ocean to the Atlantic Ocean, Delia Akeley exhibited an innate curiosity about places and peoples about which little information was known, often purposely plotting her paths to lead into unexplored regions. She once remarked, "I am always frightened in the jungle—always prepared for a violent death. But I love it!" In her pioneering work with primates she laid much of the foundation for the subsequent studies by other women, such as Jane Goodall and Dian Fossey.

Delia Denning Akeley was born on a farm in Wisconsin in 1875, the youngest of nine children. Her parents, Patrick and Margaret, were Irish Catholic immigrants and were over sixty and over forty years of age, respectively, at her birth. Dubbed "Mickey" by her family for her love of fighting with her siblings like an Irish pugilist, Delia detested rural life and particularly despised the chores and the ennui that were implicit in the day-to-day routine.

At thirteen she made an early and permanent break with her family, running away to Milwaukee, the nearest city. There she was befriended by a local barber, Arthur Reiss, who helped her procure a job as a dishwasher, ironically one of the chores she had recently attempted to escape. She and Reiss were married shortly after her fourteenth birthday.

Reiss was a weekend sportsman and often went hunting with Chicago's Field Museum of Natural History taxidermist, Carl Ethan Akeley. Although it was likely a move he would later regret, Reiss introduced Delia to Akeley. The attraction was immediate, and Delia and Carl Akeley were married in 1902, following her divorce from Reiss. Carl Akeley had gained renown in some circles for revolutionizing the art of taxidermy by employing a novel sculpting technique to create museum dioramas, stuffed groupings of formerly live animals displayed in man-made replicas of their natural habitats.

From 1905 to 1906 Delia Akeley accompanied her husband on a museum-sponsored expedition to Africa, her first foray out of the country. During the eight harrowing months in East Africa, Delia became an accomplished markswoman, although she did not believe in hunting for sport but only for food, in self-defense, or for collecting. She was convinced that varieties of wildlife were disappearing and that collecting animals by killing them and maintaining their bodies was the only way to preserve the species for viewing by future generations.

After journeying in East Africa to Kenya, the Akeleys trekked into the wilds on an elephant hunt to fulfill the museum's request for a display featuring an entire family of the massive creatures. Within two weeks of their arrival Carl bagged a large elephant but in the process of firing his gun, he excited the herd, which stampeded and nearly crushed him to death. The expedition porters fled in fear for their lives, and Delia was left alone to nurse her husband back to health. A few weeks later in the foothills of Mount Kenya, eight thousand feet up the slope, Delia downed her first elephant. In her memoir, *All True!*, she described her reaction as "scarcely breathing and with legs trembling."

While in Africa Delia Akeley acquired a love for the primates of the jungle, especially the monkeys. By observing their behavior she became convinced they had a system of language and were capable of communicating with humans. Much later, of course, her theories gained credence through the research of Jane Goodall and Dian Fossey, who may have used Akeley's initial interest as inspiration for their work. Delia Akeley "adopted" one of the monkeys, naming him "J.T." and taking him with her wherever she went. The furry creature became her charge for nine years, sleeping in her home and being treated as her child. Although destructive to her living quarters and personal property, J.T. was Delia's obsession and is memorialized in her book, *J.T., Jr.: The Biography of an African Monkey* (1929). Because the work was written from a personal perspective in lay language and not from a purely scientific point of view, it gained a wide popular audience.

During World War I Delia volunteered to do canteen work with the American Expeditionary Forces in France, where she lectured on big game hunting. Because they had been apart for some time, Carl Akeley filed for divorce in 1923, charging her with desertion; she cross-filed on grounds of cruelty and was awarded the decree. Six weeks later she was off to Africa alone, and the American press was astonished.

In October 1924, Delia Akeley, alone with male African porters and guides, trekked across the uncharted desert country between the Tana River in Kenya and Ethiopia. During the first leg of the trip, she lost thirty pounds as she journeyed astride a camel as part of a caravan; at the end of the desert region, that mode of transport was replaced by ten weeks in a dugout canoe. Parts of the territory through which she passed were Somali-ruled, and the Somalis were at war. Delia progressed through the area unscathed, for a lone woman, unaccompanied by soldiers, was perceived as no threat to the Somalis. On the trip she discovered new species of antelope and bird, collected over thirty specimens, and contributed articles to *The Saturday Evening Post, Collier's,* and *Century* magazines.

Her second expedition, underwritten by the Brooklyn Museum of Arts and Sciences, marked the first collecting jaunt ever led by a woman. She shot, preserved, and shipped mammals; accumulated regional crafts; and photographed and studied the human population of the country. One of those populations, previously virtually unexposed to the outside world, was the Pygmies in the Ituri Forest in the northeastern Belgian Congo (Zaire). She spent five months among the Pygmies, shooting over five thousand feet of film, documenting their culture, and bringing back data on their customs, diet, and stature. A later explorer working among the Pygmies noted that their chief's name was "Dee-lia," no doubt a tribute to Akeley's reputation among them.

At sixty-four years of age Delia Akeley married Dr. Warren D. Howe. The couple resided in a Daytona Beach, Florida, hotel until she died in 1970. She left an estate of $1.5 million to the heirs of the family she had abandoned over eighty years before.

Delia Akeley, although a woman of tough mettle and a minor celebrity in her own right, is rarely given credit for any of the work she did with and for Carl Akeley. Most of that merit went to Akeley's second wife, Mary Jobe, which proved contentious for Delia. On the other hand, she consistently lived life on her own terms and cut her own swath through a region dear to her.

References and Suggested Reading

McLoone, Margo. *Women Explorers in Africa*. Mankato, MN: Capstone Press, 1997.
Olds, Elizabeth Fagg. *Women of the Four Winds*. Boston: Houghton Mifflin Company, 1985.

Mary Lenore Jobe Akeley
(1878–1966)

United States
Explorer/Mountaineer

Photographer, mountaineer, and cartographer, Mary Jobe Akeley led six expeditions into the Canadian Northwest and made significant contributions to the mapping of the Canadian Rockies. With her husband, Carl Akeley, she made several circuits through Africa, taking one expedition to completion after his death.

Mary Lenore Jobe Akeley was born on a farm in Tappan, Ohio, in 1878, the daughter of Richard Watson and Sarah Jane Pitts Jobe. After graduating from Scio College in Alliance, Ohio, she taught public school until 1901, when she entered Bryn Mawr for graduate work in English and history. To help defray her educational expenses, she accepted a teaching post at Temple University in Philadelphia, while continuing to study at Bryn Mawr. After transferring to Columbia University in New York, Akeley received her master of arts in 1909 and joined the faculty of Hunter College.

There is an old adage that says those who can, do; those who cannot, teach. Mary Jobe wanted to both teach and accomplish other goals as well. By 1913 that desire compelled her to request an extended leave from her teaching post to go exploring in British Columbia, a region that had long intrigued her. She trekked through the Canadian Rockies from 1914 to 1918, studying and photographing Indian habitats and tackling the higher peaks of the region. During the period the Canadian government commissioned her to explore and map the Fraser River and applauded her attempts to be the first person to climb Mount Sir Alexander, one of the Rockies' towering ascents. By 1925 her aspiration was officially honored when the Geographic Board of Canada renamed one of the peaks Mount Jobe and recognized her mapping of the region around the mountain, which rises near the British Columbia-Alberta border, as the only valid source of information on the area at that time.

By the time her path crossed that of museum taxidermist Carl Ethan Akeley in 1918, Mary Jobe was recognized as an outstanding explorer in Canada and had been awarded membership in the American Geographical Society. Jobe and Akeley were married in 1924, a few months after his divorce from Delia, and immediately departed on safari to Africa to collect specimens of plants and animals for the Great African Hall of the American Museum of Natural History in New York City.

While in the Belgian Congo near Mount Mikeno, the Akeleys studied gorilla habitats and surveyed the protective environment of Parc National Albert as a possible sanctuary for the giant apes. Carl Akeley died suddenly in 1926, and Mary Jobe took over as leader of the expedition. She mapped areas of the Belgian Congo (Zaire), Kenya, and Tanganyika

(Tanzania); collected plants; and took hundreds of photographs, including a study of pink flamingos indigenous to sections of Uganda.

Back in New York Mary Jobe Akeley accepted an offer to become special advisor to the Great African Hall, renamed Akeley Hall in 1936, a position she held for eleven years. But one cannot be an advisor from far away, and in 1928 she welcomed an invitation from King Albert of Belgium to enlarge the gorilla park she and her husband had founded in the Congo. During that sojourn, she became a serious student of tribal customs and ceremonies, worked to protect the Pygmies in the region around Parc National Albert and crusaded for the establishment of game preserves.

In 1935 she mounted her own expedition to the Transvaal, Southern Rhodesia, and Portuguese East Africa, inspecting the wildlife in Kruger National Park and photographing the Zulus and the Swazis. Three years later, drawn by memories of her first love, she returned to British Columbia to explore the Canoe River. While there, she reviewed Alaska as a possible defense outpost for future observation, including Kodiak Island in 1941. From her work there, she created documents of interest to the United States government during World War II.

Summoned again by the Belgian aristocracy, Akeley revisited Africa in 1947 to inspect all the wildlife sanctuaries and parks in the Congo. She filmed large mammals, some nearing extinction, and helped alert the world to Africa's vanishing species. Three published works, *The Restless Jungle* (1936), *Rumble of a Distant Drum* (1946), and *Congo Eden* (1950), reflect her views on the Congo. She died in 1966 of a stroke.

Both with her husband and on her own, Mary Jobe Akeley undertook pivotal work on two continents. In Africa she aided in the salvation of endangered species, and she added significantly to the store of knowledge on the Canadian Rockies.

References and Suggested Reading

Akeley, Mary Lenore Jobe. Personal papers stored in the American Museum of Natural History, New York City.

Frost-Knappman, Elizabeth. *Women's Progress in America*. Santa Barbara, CA: ABC–CLIO, 1994.

Gilmartin, Patricia. "Mary Jobe Akeley's Exploration in the Canadian Rockies." *The Geographical Journal* (November 1990) 156: 297–304.

James, Edward T., Janet W. James, and Paul S. Boyer, eds. *Notable American Women, 1607–1950*. Cambridge, MA: Harvard University Press, 1971.

Jacqueline Marie-Therese Suzanne Douet Auriol (1917–2000)

France
Aviator

Courtesy of C. L. Osborne

In 1952 Jacqueline Auriol was the fastest woman in the world, clocking a speed of 534.375 miles per hour in a Mistral jet fighter. Although she had been seriously injured in a crash in 1949, she climbed back into the cockpit and was among the first of either gender to break the sound barrier.

Jacqueline Marie-Therese Suzanne Douet Auriol was born in 1917, in Challons, France, near the Bay of Biscay. Her father, Pierre Douet, was a shipbuilder and importer, and the young woman studied art at the Louvre School in Paris.

Through family contacts Jacqueline was introduced to Paul Auriol, the son of the future president of France. After a short acquaintance the two announced their intent to marry but that wish was immediately quashed by both families as an inappropriate match, and they were physically separated for two years. The separation failed to work, however, and they were married in 1938. As a French political wife, Jacqueline became the senior Auriol's press secretary, lived in Paris, acted as his emissary at social functions, and presented him with two grandchildren.

At the age of thirty, tiring of the party circuit and purely out of curiosity, Jacqueline Auriol took her first flight in a small plane with Commander Raymond Guillaume. She was mesmerized by the freedom of being aloft and determined to learn to fly on her own. Taking lessons in secret, she qualified as a tourist pilot in 1948. Not satisfied with a pilot's license, she approached Guillaume to teach her stunt flying. He agreed, but only with written permission from her father-in-law, which she finally managed to obtain.

In 1949 she was the only woman in a field of twenty to demonstrate her newly acquired feats before an audience of thirty thousand spectators. Three days later, however, her ambition came temporarily to a crashing halt. A seaplane in which she was a passenger nose-dived into the Seine. When she was removed from the crash, it was discovered that every bone in her face was crushed and that her skull was fractured in three places. Consequently, she spent years in hospitals and underwent more than twenty-two operations. Extended medical stays can lead to monotonous pursuits, but not for Jacqueline Auriol; she spent the months in bed consuming every work she could locate on aerodynamics.

While still undergoing treatment for her injuries, Auriol gained her license as a military pilot in 1950 and qualified for a helicopter operator's license in 1951, while she was enduring six months of plastic surgery in the United States. At Brétigny she qualified as the world's first woman test pilot, subsequently reviewing more than fifty types of aircraft for the French and breaking the speed record in 1951 in an untried Vampire jet. She held the woman's world speed record five times between 1951 and 1964 and was awarded the French Légion d'Honneur and the American Harmon Trophy in 1951 and 1953. In addition, she was among the first to break the sound barrier in 1953 and to pilot the supersonic *Concorde*.

Auriol was selected by the Ministère de la Coopération to employ remote sensing techniques that assisted agricultural development in France by mapping crop species and locating water sources for irrigation. For that endeavor she was awarded the United Nations Food and Agricultural Organization's Ceres Medal. She died in Paris in 2000.

It would have been simple for Jacqueline Auriol to function merely as part of the pampered political aristocracy of France; however, she followed her desire to soar among the eagles. In spite of intense physical pain, she became a trail blazer for women in the field of aviation.

References and Suggested Reading

Auriol, Jacqueline. *I Live to Fly*. (trans. from the French by Pamela Swinglehurst). New York: E. P. Dutton, 1970.
New York Times (obituary). 17 February 2000, C25.
xrefer Web site. "Auriol, Jacqueline." *http://www.xrefer.com/entry/359238*

Isabelle Autissier
(1956–   )

France
Sailor

Although she claims to be merely "a normal woman, doing what I like," Isabelle Autissier is hardly average. In small boats, ranging from thirty-three feet to sixty feet long, she has solo-navigated the globe two and one-half times, covering more than sixty thousand miles. That figure marks one-fourth of the distance to the moon, which is ironic since more people have flown in space than have sailed around the world alone.

Isabelle Autissier was born in the suburbs of Paris in 1956. Her father, Jean Autissier, was an architect with an abiding love of boating and for his five daughters. During summer vacations on the Brittany coast, he combined those passions and taught each of his daughters to sail, allowing Isabelle to "skipper" a wooden dinghy when she was seven years old. The Autissiers convinced each of their girls that anything they really wanted to do was possible, and Isabelle obviously took that encouragement to heart.

After graduating from the L'ecole Nationale Argonomique School in Rennes with a degree in marine engineering, Isabelle Autissier embarked on a short-lived teaching career. Her heart was not in the classroom, however, for it was her dream "to engage faraway people on a first-name basis." To that end, she taught during the day and spent three years of her nights and weekends designing and then welding together a thirty-foot steel cruising boat that she christened *Parole*. In 1977, at the age of twenty-one, she successfully navigated the boat across the Atlantic and back to France by herself. After surrendering to the freedom of the sea, Autissier regretfully resumed her post as a professor of marine science, which she called merely instructing fishermen to fish with better techniques. Although yearning for her watery wilderness, she knew that the teaching assignment would bring in enough money for her support, while allowing her the summers off to sail.

Autissier entered the racing arena as a "singlehander" officially in 1989. Until that time singlehanding (solo distance racing) was considered a male-only pursuit. When she placed third in her first outing, she immediately resigned from teaching and began actively seeking sponsors for the ultimate adventure, sailing around the world. By 1991 Isabelle Autissier had found her backers and became the first woman to circumnavigate the planet alone. She was the only distaff entrant in the twenty-seven-thousand-mile endurance test known as the BOC Challenge, named for the race sponsor, the British Oxygen Company.

Because there are so few people in the world who would consider competing in this type of contest, mapped out on such a grueling course, the around-the-world competitions are held only every four years. Even though the boats are fitted with high-tech communication devices, computers, the Internet, and voice connections to the other boats and the command post, participants in the race can anticipate approximately eight months at sea without the physical presence of another human being. On Autissier's first attempt in the BOC, the boat's mast cracked in the middle of the Indian Ocean, threatening to capsize the craft. Drawing on her now famous calm reserve, she not only refused to give up but repaired the damage and finished the sail in seventh place.

Isabelle Autissier became a national hero in France in 1994 when she and a crew of three men sailed from New York City around Cape Horn to San Francisco in sixty-two days, five hours, and fifty-five minutes, a world record for the voyage. Later that year she reentered the BOC, finishing the seven thousand-mile first leg of the voyage from Charleston, South Carolina, the traditional starting port, to Cape Town, South Africa, twelve hundred miles ahead of her nearest competitor. En route she successfully passed all seventeen of her male rivals. On the second leg, however, Mother Nature, the sailor's constant companion, refused to play fair. Fifty knot winds created monstrous waves that slung the small boat around, eventually snapping the eighty-three-foot mast like a twig. Autissier rigged a make-shift device, as she had on the previous trip, but this time her luck did not hold. The rigging plummeted again, causing the boat to list into the heaving surf. After hours of being literally upside down in the still swirling storm, she was rescued by the Australian Maritime Safety Authority, who cited it as nothing short of a miracle to have located such a small boat in such a big sea.

In 1995 Autissier entered the Vendee Globe, a competition comparable to the BOC with the rather formidable exception that participants are forbidden to stop or to seek assistance from any of the other entrants. Once again the Indian Ocean proved to be her foe as the ship's rudder broke, and she had to make landfall for repairs, an automatic disqualification.

The BOC changed its name to Around Alone in 1998 and, inevitably, Autissier was the only woman entered. By then she had gained a reputation for being a brilliant navigator. Some may have considered her exacting skill in forecasting weather the product of psychic powers unless they knew she spent two to five hours a day on her boat's Internet connection diligently researching conditions ahead. Telling the South Carolina press that, at forty-two years of age, this would be her last race, win or lose, Autissier boarded her vessel. The initial segment of the voyage was not exactly smooth sailing, and by the time the boats reached the final leg of the course, only three competitors were left, two of French origin and one Italian. One of the French captains was Isabelle Autissier and for awhile it appeared she might actually win her final competition.

Weather, no matter how well predicted, is a fickle mistress, and again it seemed to target Isabelle. Near the "Screaming Fifties," an Antarctic-influenced region nineteen hundred miles west of Cape Horn, a vicious storm appeared unannounced. While she was napping, Autissier heard the wind shift and awoke to déjà vu as she watched the ship's mast dive parallel to the water. Soon the boat capsized, rolling neatly onto its top. Isabelle barely managed to get out the SOS, "I'm upside down," before the electricity failed. Calmly, she prepared all the emergency equipment. After that, she reorganized the topsy-turvy interior in order for her craft to be as ship-shape as it normally was when it sank to the bottom of the ocean. Then she waited, standing on the ceiling of the million dollar vessel she had monitored so closely during construction.

As the waves pitched around Autissier, the distress call was channeled back to the competitor in closest proximity, her friend, Giovanni Soldini, the Italian entrant. Abandoning the course, Soldini immediately went in search of Isabelle. After hours of scanning the waves, he spotted her disabled craft and pulled alongside. With the poise that had become her trademark, Autissier opened the hatch, climbed out, and allowed the salty water to rush in, burying the vessel she loved. In one leap she swung aboard the Italian boat, holding her passport, the only memento she kept of the months at sea.

True to her word, Autissier retired from global contests and returned to her native France, where she occasionally participated in summer regattas. Although she never won a race, Isabelle Autissier is the only woman competitor in singlehanding who ever came close. The sole laurel for the winner is a silver plate which will likely never grace her mantle.

References and Suggested Reading

Adams, Susan B. "Sailing Alone at Christmas, Bombarded by Angry Seas." *New York Times*, 25 December 1998: D5.

Callihan, Steve, and Deborah Bennett. "Autissier Clobbers the Competition." *Cruising World* (January 1995) 21: 8–10.

Lloyd, Barbara. "Autissier Faces New Test." *New York Times*, 11 January 1998: D10.

———. "A New Gale Threatens Autissier." *New York Times*, 18 February 1999: D3.

———. "A Rival Plucks Sailor." *New York Times*, 17 February 1999: D2.

———. "Solo Sailor Sends Message She Capsized at Sea." *New York Times*, 16 February 1999: D1.

McCormick, Herb. "A Woman of Singular Disposition." *Cruising World* (January 1999) 25: 32–38.

"Rescue at Sea." *Sports Illustrated*, 9 January 1995, 82: 16.

Ann Bancroft
(1955–   )

United States
Arctic/Antarctic Explorer

Walking, skiing, and mushing teams of dogs across hundreds of miles of solid ice through gale-force winds and frigid temperatures is Ann Bancroft's idea of a good time. As the first woman to reach both the North Pole and the South Pole, her indomitable spirit pushes her forward through the most horrendous weather conditions and helps her manage the financial ups and downs of her career as a Pole explorer.

Ann Bancroft was born in Mendota Heights, Minnesota, in 1955. Her parents, Dick and Debby Bancroft, are both social activists; her mother was threatened with incarceration after her vocal protests over Honeywell's defense contracts, and her father, a photographer, has documented the often deplorable living conditions in Central America. Except for the two years the family spent in East Africa when she was in the fifth and sixth grades, Bancroft's childhood was spent in the Minnesota outdoors, taking long winter strolls through the snow and being taught by her brother to rappel off a frozen waterfall in her backyard when she was eleven. An early diagnosis of dyslexia reinforced her "toughening up," as she strove not to appear impaired in any way. She received a degree in physical education from the University of Oregon and taught that discipline, as well as special education, at the Clara Barton Open School in Minneapolis.

Although she had been a winter hiker all her life as well as an expert canoeist and rock climber, cresting Mount McKinley at age twenty-eight, the dramatic shift in Bancroft's path did not arrive until the mid-1980s when a family friend, Will Steger, visited her parents. Steger was on a national fund-raising jaunt to mount an expedition to the North Pole. It was a quest that had not been attempted since the 1909 expedition of Robert Peary and Matthew Henson, whose success had been challenged by historians. Several potential backers suggested, perhaps in jest, that Steger take a woman on the trek, which would be tackled by dog sled and on foot. Recalling that suggestion and being familiar with Bancroft's background, Steger asked if she would be interested in joining the expedition. For Ann Bancroft it was the realization of a childhood dream, and it took little time for her to respond with a decisive yes.

She resigned from her job and joined Steger's group for extensive training. For over a year the original seven men and one woman team lived together in tents in the woods, engaged primarily in day-to-day survival activities, such as hauling water and firewood and learning to manage teams of sled dogs. In March 1986 the eight explorers with forty-nine dogs and five loaded sleds left Ellesmere Island in northern Canada en route to the North Pole. The temperature was seventy degrees below zero, the sleds were too weighty, and the group, constantly hacking through ice and untangling the dogs, managed to cover only one mile during their first day out.

The "ground" on which they were traveling was solid ice with occasional deceptive areas of snow, and even careful observation in the near whiteout conditions could not always be counted on to discern the difference. As she ran alongside the dog sled, Bancroft accidentally stepped on one of the snow patches and plunged into the Arctic. Catching the ice shelf at the last moment, she hoisted herself out of the frigid water. At those temperatures water can be lethal, and she had to rip off her clothes, for they had instantly frozen. The group monitored her closely for the next few days for signs of hypothermia, but she miraculously escaped that threat. Two of the men were not as fortunate as she, and they had to be airlifted out due to injury and frostbite.

Realizing they could move faster with a lighter load, the group, now down to six, ditched part of their supplies and progressed at approximately twenty miles each day. Spring comes even to the Arctic, and near the end of the trek the expedition had to reroute constantly to avoid huge gaps in the ice. At last, after fifty-five days out, the compass proved they had reached the North Pole. They were the first expedition to successfully reach that part of the world without resupplying, and Ann Bancroft was launched into the national celebrity spotlight as the first woman to set foot on the North Pole.

In addition to her other duties with the group, Bancroft had served as the official photographer and cinematographer for *National Geographic*, one of the expedition's major sponsors. The magazine published her photographs along with her travel journals in September 1986. On their return the explorers were received at a White House reception in their honor and Bancroft was offered an invitation to climb Mount Everest, commentary spots on national television news, and marriage proposals.

But Bancroft heard a loftier calling. She wanted to accomplish something epic for womankind, while "shrinking the globe" for school children and educating the population about the environment. Hoping to draw backers through her current popularity, including being named one of *Ms. Magazine*'s Outstanding Women of the Year in 1988, she organized the American Women's Expedition, an undertaking that would unite women explorers from across the world to trudge the seventeen hundred miles across Antarctica, the wildest, windiest, and emptiest spot on the planet. The continent of Antarctica, 97 percent covered in thick, impregnable ice, could incorporate both the United States and Mexico. As she envisioned it, the route would move from the Filcher Ice Shelf southeast of Chile to the Ross Ice Shelf south of Australia. Although a national hero and a recognized explorer, Bancroft's expertise in raising corporate funds was not refined, and by the designated departure time she had managed to pull together only one-fourth of her projected budget. Not discouraged, the group of four women used a portion of the sponsorship monies for an April 1992 training run in Greenland and left for the icy continent in October of that year. It was summer in Antarctica, and not only did the women have to deal with the usual problems of frigid 30 degree below temperatures and persistent whiteout conditions, where the entire vista disappears into a whirling mass of snow and ice, they also had to adjust their body rhythms to the twenty-four-hour daylight present at that time of the year. By 1993 the group reached the South Pole and most, excluding Bancroft, were ready to turn back. After considering the others and weighing her options, Ann Bancroft knew she could be momentarily satisfied with being the first woman to reach both the North and South Poles, and she terminated the expedition. When she returned to the United States, however, she realized that she alone would have to deal with the mountain of debt, nearly one-half million dollars, the trip had incurred, as well as with media speculation about whether the junket would have been more successful if it had been led by a man. Even *National Geographic*, her former champion, killed the story she wrote about the trek on the basis of inferior photographs.

The next few years were spent in fund raising, giving speeches and presentations around the country, taking part in environmental public service announcements, attempting to publish children's books, and creating a documentary film on Antarctica—all in an effort to reduce her indebtedness. The one bright spot during the period was her nomination in 1995 to the National Women's Hall of Fame.

By November of 2000 Bancroft was ready to try again. With only fellow teacher Liv Arneson of Norway, the first woman to ski to the South Pole, Bancroft commenced a one-hundred-day journey across Antarctica from Queen Maud Land to the Ross Ice Shelf. As a means of promotion, The Bancroft-Arneson Expedition, with the support of National Center for Health Education (NCHE) and Base Camp Promotions, had developed and distributed a free interdisciplinary video curriculum for elementary school classrooms. To enhance this educational experience, weekly journal entries were posted via satellite and the world wide web. In January 2001 the two women once more reached the South Pole and moved on.

On day ninety-four the expedition sighted the Ross Ice Shelf, the end of the trail, and radioed for a plane pick up. There were only a few hours left for the plane to transfer them to the waiting boat that had to follow the last icebreaker out of the region or be stranded for the duration of the winter. Conditions were far from ideal, and the pilot had difficulty locating the pair until they cleverly spread out their colorful gear as a runway marker.

When they reached the ship, the Captain ordered a sumptuous meal prepared in their honor. After weeks of subsisting on dried and canned foods, the cooking aroma assailed their senses and smelled wonderful. But, for Bancroft, it was not as rich as the sweet smell of success—at last.

References and Suggested Reading

"Cool Site." *Maclean's*, 29 January 2001, 50.

"Eighteen Nominees Chosen for National Women's Hall of Fame." *The Christian Science Monitor*, 15 September 1995, 87: 4.

Jayatilleke, Ruwan. "Teach Across Antarctica." *Instructor* (October 2000) 110: 8.

Kaplan, James. "Acts of Courage: Everything Is North." *Vogue* (March 1987): 452–53.

Lindgren, Amy. "Explorer Ann Bancroft Describes Her Journey to a Fulfilling Career." *Knight-Ridder/Tribune News Service*, 2 May 2000, K4530.

Neff, Craig, and Robert Sullivan. "On Top of the World." *Sports Illustrated*, 12 May 1986, 64:13.

Tamarkin, Civia. "Mush to Her Joy, Ann Bancroft Triumphs as the First Woman to Reach the North Pole by Dogsled." *People Weekly*, 30 June 1986, 49–52.

Gertrude Margaret Lowthian Bell
(1868–1926)

England
Middle East Explorer

As a member of Britain's upper class, Gertrude Bell was expected to grow up to be a proper Victorian lady but that appeared to be an unreasonable demand on the outspoken and opinionated young woman. That brashness cultivated in her youth would hold her in good stead, however, as she tramped across the Arabian Desert, dined with sheiks and bandits, and became advisor to a variety of heads of state.

Gertrude Margaret Lowthian Bell was born in Washington Hall, County Durham, England, in 1868. She was the only daughter of prominent industrialist Sir Hugh Bell, who raised the child from three years of age, after the death of her mother. On the one hand, she was trained as a proper young woman who never walked in the city without a chaperone; at the same time, she became one of the first women in history to attend Oxford University. In 1888 she was the first woman to be awarded a degree in modern history with first-class honors from Oxford. That alone was considered a notable feat, but it was intensified by the fact that Bell challenged all of her professors' views during her oral examinations.

Following her graduation, her father, assuming it was time she married, sent Gertrude to Bucharest in care of an aunt who attempted to secure a suitable match for the vocal young woman. But Bell had other ideas, and it was those other ideas that discouraged young men from becoming her suitors. Only one of the crop intrigued her, Valentine Chirol, a foreign correspondent for the *London Times*, who eventually became her long-term confidante and counselor.

Giving up on her aunt's attempts to procure a mate for her, Bell resolved to devote herself to travel, choosing as her first destination Tehran, where her uncle, Sir Frank Lascelles, served as British ambassador. Ironically, it was there that she fell in love with a young diplomat, Henry Cadogan. Her family, however, disapproved of the match because Cadogan had a reputation as a gambler, and she was whisked back to England. While in romantic exile, she anonymously published *Safar Nemah: Persian Pictures, A Book of Travel* in 1894 and translated *Poems from the Divan of Hafiz* in 1897. A few months after her return, she was notified that Cadogan had died of pneumonia, and she immediately buried her grief and packed her trunks for her next excursion.

Still attracted by the Middle East, she taught herself Persian and went to Jerusalem to study Arabic and Farsi in 1899. After visiting Baghdad and Damascus, she set off across the Arabian Desert on horseback, penetrating regions most likely never previously viewed by a Western woman. She visited the secretive Druze and the satanic Yazidis, befriending all as she wended her way from sect to sect. According to one biographer, she so impressed the Arab leaders that they made her an "honorary man," even though she carried with her all the accoutrements of a proper lady, including fine china and crystal for dining.

Back in Europe after the turn of the century, Gertrude Bell took up mountain climbing in the Alps, and one of those gigantic, rugged elevations now bears her name. On one expedition her party was caught in an avalanche in the middle of a thunderstorm and survived only by wedging themselves in a small crevasse for several hours. In addition to cresting peaks between 1901 and 1904, she managed to squeeze in two trips around the world with her family.

The Middle East always called her back, however, and returning there, Bell traveled through Syria and Asia Minor, excavating Byzantine relics. She journeyed up the Tigris and down the Euphrates and stumbled across the ancient ruins at Ukhaidir. Although she had hoped to publish concerning this find and thus increase her academic credibility, another archaeologist published first. Her photographs and measurements were used as a supplement to his work. On the other hand, she published two books covering her journey: *Amurath to Amurath* (1911) and *The Palace and Mosque of Ukhaidir* (1914). During the jaunt, she was robbed of her money, clothes, and saddlebags, which contained her precious notebooks. Although considered a bit odd, she was liked by most of the peoples she met, and word of the theft spread among the villages. A few hours later, the bags mysteriously reappeared on a rock above her campsite.

Although she was warned by the British not to go and she had not asked permission from the Turks, Gertrude Bell set out from Damascus in 1913 to wander the northernmost sections of the Arabian Desert, an area untouched by Westerners for over twenty years. She reached the walled city of Hail, a hotbed of political disturbance, where she was greeted by the uncle of the young emir and offered the guest house on palace grounds. When she awoke the next morning, she discovered her things had been confiscated as a means of detaining her, and she remained a virtual prisoner on the grounds for eleven days. Eventually, she talked her way out, but she did not find out until later how valuable this trip and the information gained during it would be.

In 1914 Bell went to France to join the Red Cross as a nurse and subsequently organized its London headquarters, which specialized in tracing missing soldiers. As a noted expert on the Middle East and as a consequence of her unsanctioned travels in Damascus, wherein she had mapped routes and water sources and had noted which groups were friendly to the British and which were not, she was asked by the British government in 1915 to join the Arab Intelligence Bureau in Cairo to collect information to be used in mobilizing the Arabs against Turkey. She settled in Baghdad in 1916, the only woman in the British Expeditionary Force in Mesopotamia. Ultimately, she was named assistant political officer in Iraq. Bell believed in Arab self-determination, predicted the inevitable union of Arab states, and was instrumental in bringing the Hashimite ruler King Faisal to the Iraqi throne in 1921. She published *The Arab of Mesopotamia* (1917) and the influential *Review of the Civil Administration in Mesopotamia* (1921), an official report on the administration of Mesopotamia between the armistice of 1918 and the Iraqi rebellion of 1920. By the early part of the 1920s, she was considered one of the most powerful women in Britain, was an advisor to heads of state, and was the only woman out of forty persons invited by Winston Churchill to a 1921 summit.

Returning to Iraq, she gained King Faisal's permission to write laws controlling the country's antiquities, assuring that excavations would stay in their country of origin, and founded the National Museum in Baghdad where she served as director of antiquities from 1923 to 1926. Despite her fame and international acclaim, Bell became despondent in her later years, and in 1926 she ingested a fatal dose of sleeping pills. She was buried in Iraq with the highest military honors.

References and Suggested Reading

O'Brien, Rosemary, ed. (with photographs by Gertrude Bell). *The Arabian Diaries*. Syracuse, NY: Syracuse University Press, 2000.

Robinson, Jane. *Wayward Women: A Guide to Women Travellers*. New York: Oxford University Press, 1990.

Uglow, Jennifer S. *The International Dictionary of Women's Biography*. New York: Continuum Press, 1982.

Wallach, Janet. *Desert Queen: The Extraordinary Life of Gertrude Bell*. New York: Doubleday, 1996.

Ruth Fulton Benedict
(1887–1948)

United States
Anthropologist

Courtesy of the Library of Congress

A lthough her personal explorations were geographically limited, Ruth Benedict was responsible for motivating hundreds of students to go into the field and for making anthropology accessible to the lay person. From her studies of indigenous populations to her work on racial disparity, Benedict earned the title of foremost woman in the field of anthropology.

Ruth Fulton Benedict was born in New York in 1887. Her father, Frederick S. Fulton, a surgeon, died suddenly when Ruth was around two years old, an event which had a lasting impact on her family. Her mother, Beatrice Shattuck Fulton, lived for years in what Benedict called "her cult of grief," as she shuttled Ruth and her sister Margery from New York to Missouri to Minnesota and back to New York, seeking employment. Coupled with the instability of this lifestyle, Benedict was diagnosed as partially deaf in 1895, which accounted in part for her withdrawal into a fantasy world as a child and a young adult.

That imaginary existence, born of a need for control, translated to paper as poetry, sometimes under the pseudonym of Ann Singleton, and led Benedict to Vassar College, her mother's alma mater, as a major in English literature. After graduation in 1909, having been elected to Phi Beta Kappa, Benedict toured Europe and then returned to Buffalo, New York, as a social worker, a profession for which she felt unsuited. Still seeking her niche, she accepted a teaching post in Los Angeles, where she met Stanley Benedict, a biochemist at the Cornell Medical College in New York City. The two were married in 1914 and moved once again to New York. After Stanley was injured in a laboratory accident and Ruth learned she was infertile, the couple began to drift apart, and she decided to return to school. In 1919 she took classes first at Columbia under John Dewey and then at The New School for Social Research, where she enrolled in ethnology courses taught by Elsie Clews Parsons. Classroom discussions kindled an interest in anthropology, which led her to enroll in Columbia University at the age of thirty-four to study under the legendary Franz Boas.

Boas became her mentor and father figure; in fact, she called him "Papa Franz." With his encouragement and some manipulation of requirements, she completed her studies in a little over a year and was awarded her doctorate in anthropology. In 1922 she accepted a teaching post at Barnard College, where she met a young psychology student, Margaret Mead, who would become her lifelong friend. Over the next four years Benedict conducted an extensive study of Native Americans in the Southwest and the northern Pacific islands, which became the basis of her theory of culture. Interested in religion and myth, she spent time with the Pueblo, Apache, Blackfeet, Serrano, and Zuni tribes, noting the differences in temperament among the groups.

On the home front Stanley Benedict was not enthusiastic about his wife's "taking up a profession," and after sixteen years of marriage the couple separated in 1931. Although at the time she had taught at Columbia for over nine years, she had never received a salary because her husband's income was considered sufficient to support them. Following the separation, she became an assistant professor assigned to Boas, her first regular faculty appointment.

In 1934 Benedict published her seminal work, *Patterns of Culture*, which became a best-seller and remains one of the most widely read books in the social sciences, essentially because it simplifies the study of culture for the lay person. In contrasting three Native American cultures, Ruth Benedict hoped to illustrate what she considered characteristics, both positive and negative, of the whole of American life.

When Boas retired in 1936, Benedict was appointed as acting executive director of the Department of Anthropology at Columbia. Over the next few years she produced *Race: Science and Politics* (1940), which refuted claims of the racial superiority of certain groups over others. She also joined the Committee for National Morale to study morale building during wartime and founded The Institute for Intercultural Studies. Through the institute she was asked to compile information on European and Asian cultures to be used by the Department of War and Office of Information when dealing with peoples in occupied territories, such as Romania, The Netherlands, Thailand, and Japan. Eventually, she concentrated on Japan, piecing together information from propaganda films, diaries, and privileged facts supplied by the United States government. From this work she produced her second best-seller, *The Chrysanthemum and The Sword: Patterns of Japanese Culture*, published in 1946 and still in print.

In 1946 Benedict received the Annual Achievement Award of the American Association of University Women, and in 1947 she was elected president of the American Anthropological Association. During that period, she was awarded a $100,000 grant to initiate the Columbia University Research in Contemporary Cultures project. Through that project, which lasted from 1947 to 1951, Benedict was instrumental in sending over one hundred twenty participants to work in seven different cultures from New Guinea and Fiji to Africa and South America.

In 1948 Benedict was at last given the one sought-after recognition that had been so elusive. She was awarded a full professorship at Columbia, the pinnacle of academic success. Unfortunately, she did not get to enjoy the promotion. She died in 1948 of a coronary thrombosis prior to the start of the fall term. Even though the majority of her exploration was done vicariously, Ruth Benedict was responsible for inspiring hundreds of young women and men to study anthropology.

References and Suggested Reading

Benedict, Ruth. Papers archived at Vassar College

Caffrey, Margaret. *Ruth Benedict: Stranger in This Land*. Austin: University of Texas Press, 1989.

Mead, Margaret. *Ruth Benedict*. New York: Columbia University Press, 1974.

Gertrude Benham
(1867–1938)

England
Mountaineer/Explorer

Mountaineer and hiker extraordinaire, Gertrude Benham conquered mountains on almost every continent and spent more than thirty years of her life literally walking the world, often into regions where no Western woman had ever been. In all, it has been estimated that she walked around the globe more than seven times.

Gertrude Benham was born in London, the youngest of six children. When she was a young woman, her father took her on a holiday in the Alps, where the two climbed Mount Blanc and the Matterhorn. Hooked on the rarefied air, she returned to Switzerland seventeen times to perfect her skill. By 1904 Benham was ready for new challenges and determined to take on the Canadian Rockies. Despite strong winds, heavy snows, rock slides, and forest fires, she ascended Mount Alberta, one of the first women to do so. Refusing to stop before reaching the summit, Benham and her party climbed at night, using only lanterns to guide their way. From there she undertook a climb of Mount Assiniboine in British Columbia and became the first woman to scale the twelve-thousand-foot peak.

Eager for more, Benham trekked through New Zealand, Japan, Nepal, and Africa. Africa's Mount Kilimanjaro, the over nineteen-thousand-foot challenge to every climber, became Gertrude Benham's next conquest. On the way up the mountain the party stumbled upon skeletons of other unfortunate climbers and the porters, frightened by this discovery, begged to turn back. Undeterred, Benham trudged on and humbled by her courage, the porters followed. As a result she added the first woman to climb Mount Kilimanjaro to her list of laurels.

In 1908 Benham walked across South America from Valparíso, Chile, to Buenos Aires, Argentina. She then crossed the Atlantic, where she crossed Kenya, covering over two thousand miles by 1911. Traversing the African continent from west to east, she spent eleven months covering more than thirty-seven hundred miles on foot. During all of her adventuring, Gertrude Benham never carried a weapon. She was armed with only a Bible, the complete works of Shakespeare, a tattered copy of *Lorna Doone*, Rudyard Kipling's *Kim*, and her knitting. The people she met may have considered her strange, but she never encountered any serious difficulty in any of her travels.

Wherever she went, she drew pictures of the mountains, which were later used in mapping; collected wild flowers, including more than eleven thousand varieties in the Himalayas; and accumulated curios from the people she met along the way. She always traveled alone or with native guides, and she managed to wander wherever she chose, spending less than 250 British pounds per year.

Benham was named a fellow of the Royal Geographic Society in 1916 and given membership in the Ladies Alpine Club of England in 1935. She died on board ship en route from Africa to England in 1938. Her vast collection of artifacts and flower specimens were left to the Plymouth City Museum in Plymouth, England.

References and Suggested Reading

Adelman, Joseph. *Famous Women*. New York: Ellis Lonow Company, 1926.
Macksey, Joan, and Kenneth Macksey. *The Guinness Guide to Feminine Achievement*. Enfield, England: Guinness Superlatives, Ltd., 1975.

Isabella Lucy Bird Bishop
(1831–1904)

Scotland
Explorer

One of the most intrepid, plucky, and prolific of lady Victorian travelers, Isabella Bishop wandered the world alone or as the lone woman in the company of men, from the rugged Western United States, to the Middle East and Far East, and to parts in between. She was celebrated as a horsewoman by those on the frontier and as a chronicler of a shrinking world by those at home.

Isabella Lucy Bird Bishop was born in Boroughbridge, Yorkshire, England, in 1831. Her father, Edward Bird, was a clergyman of the Church of England, and her mother, Dora Lawson Bird, was a minister's daughter. In an atmosphere of strict religiosity and moral rigor, Isabella and her sister Henrietta were taught at home. Among the skills her father instilled in the girls was how to ride a horse properly. Diagnosed with a spinal illness, a popular catch phrase for a variety of ailments at the time, Isabella was prescribed extensive horseback riding and swimming as therapy. When those pursuits failed to lift her malaise, the doctor recommended travel by sea. In 1854 she made her first voyage to the United States, which restored her health and culminated in the publication of her first work, *The Englishwoman in America* (1856). This trip also set Bishop on a life path from which she never deviated.

In 1858 Edward Bird died and Isabella, Henrietta, and their mother moved to Edinburgh, Scotland. Isabella became concerned with the urban and rural poverty of the area and aided Scots who hoped to immigrate to Canada. After the death of her mother Isabella, declining an invitation to stay with her sister, packed her trunks and was off again. In 1873 she undertook an eighteen-month tour of Australia, New Zealand, the Pacific Islands, and the United States. En route she fell in love with the climate and topography of the Sandwich Islands, better known as Hawaii, and remained there for six months. She studied the religious practices of the natives, toured a leper colony, and spent a night camping on the rim of Mauna Loa volcano as lava bubbled beneath her.

From Hawaii she sailed to San Francisco and made her way on horseback eastward to the Rocky Mountains. There she met and fell in love with an unlikely character known as Mountain Jim. Jim Nugent was an alcoholic, a gun-for-hire, and fifteen years older than Isabella. They were an odd but perfect match; he was taken by her spunk, and she was awed by his romantic gentleness. She persuaded him to act as a guide for her climb of Long's Peak, the highest mountain in the region at three thousand feet. For years she had endeavored to become a fellow of the Royal Geographical Society, which at the time did not accept women for membership. It was her impression that the more "firsts" she could rack up, the better her chances were for becoming the initial woman invited to join the Society.

Mountain Jim agreed to the climb, which they commenced in late fall under rather risky weather conditions. Tired and cold, Isabella made it to the top. On the descent, however, she lost her footing and began sliding down the mountain, but fortunately her dress snagged on a rock, leaving her dangling in mid-air. Jim sliced the dress away with his hunting knife, and Isabella plummeted into a crevice filled with soft snow. After the rescue she stayed in the area, known as Estes Park, for some time, living in a cabin, where she was often snowed in with Mountain Jim and his ranch hands. Occasionally Isabella helped with the chores around the property and especially enjoyed rounding up the cattle and working in the barn. After several months Isabella was running short of funds and, despite Jim's awkward marriage proposal, she returned to Scotland. Later she learned that the gentle outlaw had been killed in a shoot-out only a few weeks after her departure. From her experiences on that outing Bishop published *The Hawaiian Archipelago* (1875) and *A Lady's Life in the Rockies* (1879). Both were well received and established her place as the most popular travel writer in Victorian England.

In 1878 Isabella Bishop toured Japan, Indonesia, and the Middle East. She spent eighteen months of that time recording the culture of the Hairy Ainu, a village of aboriginal Japanese. After being notified that her sister was seriously ill, she returned to Scotland in 1881 to care for Henrietta until her death. Although she had previously rejected him, Isabella, at age fifty and with some trepidation, accepted the marriage proposal of Dr. John Bishop, her sister's physician, on the condition that she be allowed to continue her travels.

Only five years later John Bishop died, and Isabella, having heard of the horrendous conditions in India, studied medicine in London and left for India as a medical missionary. She founded two hospitals in the Punjab and Kashmir and named them for her husband and her sister, respectively. From there she went by boat up the Yangtze River, where she developed her photographs in the murky river water. She continued overland in a carrying chair. Traveling over eight thousand miles alone, she penetrated through Szechwan to the Tibetan border, farther than any white woman had ever been before. Across Tibet, through Afghanistan and Persia to the Black Sea, to Kurdistan, Korea, and China, she pushed onward, despite ridicule from the locals for being unaccompanied by a husband, and founded three more hospitals during her five-year pilgrimage.

In 1892 Isabella Bird Bishop received the recognition she had desired for such a long time. She was named the first woman fellow of the Royal Geographical Society. Her last fling was a one-thousand-mile ride, at the age of seventy, across Morocco on a stallion she had to mount by stepladder. She died in Edinburgh of cancer in 1904 with her thirteen travel books lined neatly on her shelf and her trunks packed and ready for her next adventure. Few people could say they had lived a fuller life.

References and Suggested Reading

Middleton, Dorothy. *Victorian Lady Travelers*. New York: E. P. Dutton and Company, 1965.

Uglow, Jennifer S. *The International Dictionary of Women's Biography*. New York: Continuum Press, 1982.

Arlene Blum
(1945–   )

United States
Mountaineer

Arlene Blum personifies energy and ambition. Her drive has taken her from scientific research in the area of environmentally hazardous chemicals to organizing an all-woman assault on the Himalayas. She teaches university courses on trekking, she organizes and guides expeditions, she lectures all over the world, and she writes books on climbing the Earth's highest peaks.

Arlene Blum was born in the Midwest, the only child of a physician and a musician who divorced soon after her birth. Shuttled off to Chicago, the young girl was raised by her maternal grandparents. Although her original ambition was to teach kindergarten, she became intrigued by the sciences in high school and majored in physical chemistry at Reed College in Oregon. While in college, Blum gazed longingly at the mountain crests ringing the campus, and after taking a basic climbing course she made numerous ascents of Oregon's volcanic peaks. For her undergraduate thesis she analyzed the volcanic gases erupting from Mount Hood, which, of course, she had to climb to observe.

While taking graduate courses in chemistry, Blum took advantage of each school break to trek off to new and higher peaks from Mexico to the Andes in South America. Needing a greater challenge, she applied to join an expedition to Afghanistan but was rejected because the organizer viewed a party of nine men and one woman as inappropriate and a deterrent to the "easy masculine companionship" that was vital to the success of the expedition. Next she offered to sponsor a trip up Alaska's Mount McKinley but was politely informed that she would not be allowed to climb higher than base camp in spite of her having more experience than most of the men accepted for the climb. Having had enough of this obvious discrimination, Blum became determined to organize her own expedition and called on her friends, both male and female, to join her. Although there was an outpouring of initial interest from both genders, gradually the men dropped out. Five women, however, accepted the challenge, and the all-woman team reached the 20,320-foot summit of Mount McKinley in the summer of 1970.

While completing her doctorate at Berkeley in 1976, Blum researched toxic chemicals and their effects on the environment. She became particularly interested in flame-retardant materials and discovered that Tris, a popular fireproofing chemical used primarily on children's pajamas, was carcinogenic. After she published the results of her experiments, the Consumer Product Safety Commission banned the use of Tris in the United States.

As opportunities arrived, she continued to climb and traveled to Afghanistan, Africa, and Nepal to seek out the sheerest cliffs. In 1976 she joined the American Bicentennial Expedition to Mount Everest, where she helped demonstrate women's stamina at high altitudes. While preparing her dissertation, conducting scientific experiments, and trekking around the globe, she plotted her grandest adventure, an all-woman team scaling of Nepal's 26,545-foot Annapurna I, the tenth highest peak in the world. Annapurna toys with those who try to climb her. With unpredictable weather and a tendency to avalanches, the mountain had allowed only four to reach the summit, while sentencing seven others to their deaths. No woman and no American had ever tried to tame the mountain.

Members of the expedition raised their own funds to cover the $80,000 estimated cost of the climb by selling T-shirts that read, "A Woman's Place Is On Top . . . Annapurna." In 1978 ten women and a technical crew boarded a plane for Nepal. Rather than attempting the summit herself, Blum felt she would be more useful in orchestrating the ascent from a series of base camps. After two months of effort, two of the women, Vera Komarkova and Irene Miller, accompanied by two Sherpas, jubilantly reached the top. Two days later, during a second attempt, two of the climbers, Vera Watson and Alison Chadwick-Onyszkiewicz, were caught in a rock slide and both died, a tragedy that caused Arlene Blum enormous remorse. The media and male-dominated climbing societies stressed the deaths, while de-emphasizing the initial success, and many attributed the accident to the weaknesses of women.

Although she gave up her scientific laboratory for a global laboratory, Arlene Blum has no regrets. She continues to divide her time between her own climbs, including the Himalayas, teaching others how to climb, and leading expeditions into the field. In 1980 she led the successful Indian-American Women's Expedition to the Gangotri Glacier near the borders of India and Tibet.

References and Suggested Reading

Blum, Arlene. *Annapurna: A Woman's Place*. San Francisco: Sierra Club Books, 1980.
De Silva, Rachel. *Leading Out: Mountaineering Stories of Adventurous Women*. Seattle: Seal Press, 1998.

Margaret Bourke-White
(1906–1971)

United States
Photographer

Courtesy of the Library of Congress

T o the eye of a photographer, forms, shapes, and colors often reveal a kind of beauty not always discernible to the layman. For a young Margaret Bourke-White, beauty was evidenced in the industrial and technological architecture consuming the cities of the United States. As she matured, both as a woman and an artist, she captured the character displayed on the faces of many of the nation's downtrodden.

Margaret Bourke-White was born in New York City in 1906. Her father, Joseph White, was a printing designer and amateur photographer; her mother, Minnie Elizabeth Bourke, published books for the blind. Both of her parents were strong believers in education, and the young woman was pressured to excel in school. As a teenager she created and sold photographic postcards while working as a camp counselor, and she contributed photographs to her high school yearbook.

Initially expressing an interest in both engineering and biology, Bourke-White attended the University of Michigan in Ann Arbor at seventeen. In 1925 she met and married a fellow engineering student, Everett Chapman, but both were highly emotional, and the marriage survived only one year. Returning East after the divorce, she entered Cornell and following the death of her father, she worked her way through school as a photographer, earning her bachelor of arts degree in 1927.

Intrigued by technology, Bourke-White attended Case Western Reserve University in Cleveland, Ohio, a growing industrial center. Working with what she called the "machine aesthetic," and drawing upon the beauty she perceived in modern technology, the young woman began to specialize in photographs of architectural and industrial subjects. Her unique arrangements and her detailed approach to subject matter gained national attention, and in 1929 publishing magnet Henry Luce asked her to do the first cover of his soon-to-be-launched *Fortune* magazine. A short time later she joined the publication as staff photographer for six months each year, while working the other six months as a successful freelancer. She served as associate editor of *Fortune* from 1929 to 1933.

In 1930 Bourke-White traveled to the Soviet Union on assignment, where she worked with a crew to create two films, *Eyes on Russia* (1931) and *Red Republic* (1934), the first travelogues to be sanctioned by the Soviet government. In addition to the documentaries she snapped over eight hundred still photos of Russian culture, a result of her growing interest in social and political causes.

Based in part on her work with the 1934 drought in the Dakotas,

Bourke-White was assigned to cover the effects of the Depression on people living in the Dust Bowl for Luce's new venture, *Life* magazine. Paired with writer Erskine Caldwell, Margaret traveled from South Carolina to Arkansas to Louisiana. It was her first real work in portraiture, and in the etched faces of the poverty stricken, she saw the same beauty she had witnessed in the sharp angles and lines and curves present in architectural embellishment. She and Caldwell co-published the results of their travels in *You Have Seen Their Faces* (1937). Her photograph of dam construction in New Deal, Montana, graced the cover of the first issue of *Life* on November 23, 1936, and was coupled with an internal spread on people in nearby towns whose life would be changed by the dam construction. It was her first effort to combine architectural forms and human emotion.

In 1939 she married Erskine Caldwell. They traveled to London, Romania, Istanbul, and Egypt, gathering materials for other co-publishing ventures. In Istanbul Bourke-White was arrested for taking photographs in a Moslem Temple during a prayer meeting, and in Beirut she learned the fine art of riding a camel. From their travels Bourke-White and Caldwell published *North of the Danube* (1939), which featured sixty-four of her photographs that are often considered her best work, and *Say, Is This the U.S.A.?* (1941), a portrait of the United States prior to World War II. After three tumultuous years, the couple divorced.

During World War II Bourke-White covered the German attack on Moscow in 1941 as the only foreign photographer in the Soviet Union. From there she was commissioned by the Army Air Force to document the action in Italy and Northern Africa, the first woman to be assigned to such a mission. She was denied permission to travel to the front with the men; thus, she went by separate ship, only to be attacked by torpedoes near North Africa. In 1945 she was attached to General George S. Patton's Third Army, one of the first groups to enter concentration camps such as Buchenwald during the last days of the Third Reich.

After the armistice she traveled to India to take carefully staged portraits of Ghandi and to South Africa and Korea to document the human aspects of guerilla warfare. She took photographs in twenty-one countries, including the Arctic, and produced a photo mural for NBC in Rockefeller Center in 1933.

She died in 1971 from Parkinson's disease but not before she made Henry Luce promise that she would be assigned to the first commercial trip to the moon. Had she lived, she would have likely done just that.

References and Suggested Reading

Bourke-White, Margaret. *Portrait of Myself.* New York: Simon and Schuster, 1963.
Brown, Theodore M. *Margaret Bourke-White, Photojournalist.* Ithaca, NY: Cornell University Press, 1972.
New York Times (obituary). 28 August 1971, 1: 3.
Rubin, Susan Goldman. *Margaret Bourke-White: Her Pictures Were Her Life.* New York: Harry N. Abrams, 1999.

Louise Arner Boyd
(1887–1972)

United States
Arctic Explorer

Courtesy of the Library of Congress

Always fascinated by the vast regions of the frozen North, Louise Arner Boyd helped open exploration as a field for women, while increasing knowledge of the Arctic lands and glacier formations. Using her own money, she chartered ships and led expeditions into Iceland, Greenland, and Lapland to bring back information later used to understand and map those little known regions.

Louise Arner Boyd was born in San Rafael, California, near San Francisco, in 1887. Her father, John Franklin Cook Boyd, was a mining operator and investor and her mother, Louise Arner Boyd, was a socialite. Since money was not an issue for the family, young Louise was educated in private schools in San Francisco, where she learned to shoot a weapon and ride a horse.

In 1920 her father died and Louise inherited the family fortune, becoming president in absentia of Boyd Investment Company. She spent the next few years traveling in Europe and first visited the Arctic regions on board a Norwegian cruise ship in 1924. She immediately fell in love with that frozen wasteland, and in 1926 Boyd chartered a ship for several of her friends and six researchers she brought along to study the flora and fauna of the area. Cruising from Norway into the Arctic Ocean, they arrived in Franz Josef Land, the island chain north of Russia, where they disembarked to hunt polar bears and seals. In addition to handling the photography, the surveying, and the planning of the expedition, Boyd bagged twenty-nine polar bears by herself.

On a return trip to the Arctic in 1928, Louise heard the news that famed South Pole explorer Roald Amundson had disappeared while flying a rescue mission to search for another missing explorer, Umberto Nobile. She immediately offered her ship as part of the rescue mission, forfeiting her own exploration as well as her own funds. After covering over ten thousand miles of Arctic Ocean, she finally gave up finding the missing hero but in the process she became a hero herself. For her efforts in the search she was awarded the Order of Saint Olaf by Norway and named Chevalier of the French Legion of Honor.

From 1931 to 1938 Boyd led a series of annual expeditions into the Arctic to conduct geological, botanical, and meteorological studies. One of the voyages examined glaciers on the northeast coast of Greenland, and she was the first to sail to the ends of that country's Ice Fjords, including the little known De Geer Glacier. In honor of her discoveries the Danish government later named the region around the glacier Louise A. Boyd Land. In 1933 the American Geographic Society funded her exploration, presenting her with a sonic device for measuring the ocean depth. After two measuring excursions Boyd and her crew reported the existence of an undiscovered undersea mountain range on the ocean floor. By 1938 she had traveled farther along the coast of Greenland than any other American had ever gone by sea. In addition, the American Geographic Society published two of her books, *The Fjord Regions of East Greenland* (1935) and *The Coast of Northeast Greenland* (1949).

World War II temporarily halted her expeditions, but in 1941 the United States government asked her to return to her beloved part of the world. The National Bureau of Standards wanted her to investigate the effects of polar magnetism on radio phenomena in Greenland. For fifteen months she was assigned to the War Department as a technical expert on military strategy in the Arctic. In 1949 the United States Army awarded her a Certificate of Appreciation.

In 1955, at the age of sixty-eight, Louise Arner Boyd returned to the Arctic, this time chartering a plane. Accustomed to traveling by water, she boarded the aircraft with some trepidation, but in the process she became the first woman to fly over and around the North Pole, snapping photographs from the plane's window. She was elected to the American Geographical Society's policy-making board in 1960, the first woman to hold such an office in the society's one-hundred-eight-year history. In 1956 the Society established the Louise A. Boyd publishing fund.

References and Suggested Reading

Anema, Durlynn. *Louise Arner Boyd: Arctic Explorer*. New York: Morgan Reynolds, 2000.

Olds, Elizabeth Fagg. *Women of the Four Winds*. Boston: Houghton Mifflin, 1985.

Susan Butcher
(1954–   )

————————————————————————➤

United States
Iditarod Champion

A lthough it was not necessarily her intention to prove that women have as much endurance and a stronger tolerance for pain than men, Susan Butcher has repeatedly done so by engaging in one of the most demanding contests on Earth, the Iditarod, a sled dog race from Anchorage to Nome, Alaska. She has established herself as number one musher in the world by breaking nine speed records in international races, including the Iditarod, where she is one of only two who have at least four first-place finishes.

Susan Butcher was born in Cambridge, Massachusetts, in 1954. Her father, Charlie, is the chairman of a chemical company and her mother, Agnes, a psychiatric social worker. From her earliest memories Susan hated life in the city, and the independent young woman escaped to the country at every opportunity. When she was fifteen, a relative gave her a Husky puppy, and Susan spent hours with the dog, preferring its company to that of other children. As soon as she got enough money, she purchased a second Husky, but her mother said the house was not big enough and one would have to go. The one who went was Susan; taking both dogs, she moved to Maine to live with her grandmother. At age sixteen she applied to a Maine boat-building school but her application was denied because her potential employer considered it an unsuitable occupation for a young woman.

When she turned eighteen, Susan Butcher packed her things and her dogs and headed West, seeking a profession that would match her love for animals and her attachment to the Huskies. Stopping first in Boulder, Colorado, she took a job as a veterinary assistant and began practicing to become a "musher," the term applied to the driver of teams of sled dogs. The way in which races were organized in Colorado was too lax for Butcher, and she realized that if she planned to become a true musher, she needed to be where the sport was considered a serious profession.

In 1975 that opportunity presented itself when Butcher was hired by the University of Alaska to work on an environmental project to save endangered musk oxen. After purchasing three more dogs she moved into an isolated cabin in the Wrangell Mountains to be near the project site and to have enough space to train the Huskies. Two years later the project and Butcher moved to Unalakleet, Alaska, where she was introduced to Joe Reddington, Sr., the organizer of the Iditarod. Reddington helped her to find her first sponsor and enter her first race, which she finished in nineteenth place, close enough to the front to convince Butcher that this was where she belonged.

The Iditarod is held annually in March. At that time of the year the route from Anchorage to Nome encompasses 1,158 miles of icy tundra, two mountains, the Bering Sea, unpredictable blizzards, temperatures to 50 degrees below zero, and winds surging up to 140 miles per hour. Each musher has a team of seven to twenty dogs, and throughout most of the race the driver is running behind the team. Although drivers are required to rest each day, most of that time is spent in maintaining the sled and caring for the dogs; consequently, sleep deprivation is often more of a problem than the threat of hypothermia.

In 1979 with Reddington Susan Butcher led the only sled dog team ever to reach the over twenty-thousand-foot summit of Mount McKinley. Although the trip took forty-four days, Butcher was confident of success, placing most of that trust in her animals, which she trains from birth to be both racers and house pets.

After reentering the Iditarod every year Susan Butcher was convinced in 1985 that she would be the first-place finisher. She had the best team of "athletes" ever assembled and was in excellent physical shape herself. As the race began, both dogs and musher were moving smoothly and well ahead of the other competitors until they came face to face with a pregnant moose. Expecting the moose to be frightened away by the dogs, Butcher stopped the team, but to her surprise, the huge animal charged the sled. Wielding an axe, the only weapon she had, Butcher kept the moose from trampling her to death until another racer arrived and shot the creature. When it was all over, however, one dog was dead, another was near death, and Butcher was suffering from physical and mental exhaustion. Loading the dead and wounded dogs onto the sled, she moved on to the next check point before dropping out of the race.

A study in persistence, she finally won the competition in 1986; won back-to-back in 1987; and became the first person to win three in a row in 1988. She set a speed record of eleven days and two hours in 1990 to win her fourth race in spite of the deepest snow in twenty-five years and the threat of volcanic activity. During that racing season Susan Butcher chalked up 2,680 miles, more than any other musher in history. Since 1984 she has placed first in ten of the eighteen long-distance races she has entered, and in 1993 she broke her own Iditarod speed record but failed to win the race.

Despite occasionally crashing into trees, being stranded in isolated regions, having bouts of hypothermia, and being attacked by a pregnant moose, Susan Butcher is doing what she loves. In 1985 she married David Monson, an attorney and fellow musher. They own and operate Trail Breaker Kennels in Eureka, Alaska, the home of over one hundred fifty huskies. These house pets consume over $30,000 worth of dog food each year. In the summers, when she cannot run the dogs twenty miles each day, she travels throughout the United States and lectures on her sport.

She has been elected the Female Athlete of the Year and was named the Top Professional Sports Woman in 1990.

References and Suggested Reading

Anchorage Daily News Web site. "Susan Butcher." *http://anchoragedailynews@ theiditarod*

InterSpeak Web site. "Susan Butcher." *http://info@inter-speak.com*

Skow, John. "Here's One Musher Who Is No Lazy Susan." *Sports Illustrated*, 15 February 1988, 68: 8–10.

Szirak, Candice. "An Intense Drive." *Women's Sports and Fitness* (March 1989) 11: 66–68.

Rachel Louise Carson
(1907–1964)

United States
Environmentalist

Courtesy of the Library of Congress

A quatic biologist Rachel Carson could be called the mother of the environmental movement. With the publication in 1962 of *Silent Spring*, her exposé of industrial pollution, she provoked not only a national outcry but a stream of negative propaganda directed against her personally by megalith chemical companies.

Rachel Louise Carson was born in Springdale, Pennsylvania, in 1907. Her father, Robert Warden Carson, was an insurance salesman and her mother, Maria McLean, was a teacher with a deep love of nature. Rachel was educated at the Pennsylvania College for Women at Pittsburgh, later Chatham University. Interested in becoming a writer, she enrolled as an English major. However, a growing interest in biology led her to change her major, despite the strong prejudices of that time against women in the sciences. After graduating magna cum laude in 1929, she enrolled at Johns Hopkins University, earning a master of arts in 1932.

For several years Carson worked in genetics and zoology as a faculty member at the University of Maryland. Gradually, however, her interests became more focused on natural history, especially through her postgraduate studies of offshore life at the Marine Biological Laboratory at Woods Hole, Massachusetts.

In 1936 she was offered a position with the United States Bureau of Fisheries as an aquatic biologist, one of the first of only two women hired by that agency in roles other than clerks. In 1937 her first major piece of writing, "Undersea," was published in *The Atlantic Monthly*, and her premier book, *Under the Sea Wind*, came out in 1941. Following World War II, she was commissioned to produce twelve illustrated booklets on National Wildlife Refuges, which set a new standard for government publications. By 1949 she had been named editor-in-chief of the American Fish and Wildlife Services and had published *The Sea Around Us* (1951) and *The Edge of the Sea* (1955), which gained her international renown.

In 1951 Carson received a Guggenheim award and built a cottage in West Southport, Maine, near the tide pools she regularly studied. After her favorite niece died Carson adopted her son, Roger. When life with Roger settled down, she began writing her magnum opus. Although she had been concerned with environmental issues for over twenty years and had even had a series of articles on the topic rejected by *Reader's Digest*, she was not prepared for the ire she was about to evoke. *Silent Spring* had advance sales of forty thousand on the day it was published and, overnight, Rachel Carson became a household name.

The book, which exposed the destruction caused by synthetic pesticides, particularly DDT, on the environment, wildlife, and humans, shot to the top of the best-seller list, was named outstanding book of the year in a *New York Times* poll, and was eventually published in thirty-two languages. But it was not the popularity of the work that Carson found overwhelming; it was the personal attacks levied at her by the agricultural and chemical industries. Through a barrage of negative propaganda and misinformation, companies labeled her a spinster, a communist, a lesbian, a scientific charlatan, or downright un-American.

Rachel Carson was vindicated when, shortly before her death of bone cancer in 1964, she was called to testify before Congress. That testimony resulted in President John F. Kennedy establishing a panel within the President's Science Advisory Committee to study the use of pesticides and their effects on the environment.

References and Suggested Reading

Brooks, Paul. *Rachel Carson: The Writer at Work*. San Francisco: Sierra Club Books, 1989.

Lear, Linda. *Rachel Carson: The Life of the Author of Silent Spring*. London: The Penguin Press, 1997.

Uglow, Jennifer S. *The International Dictionary of Women's Biography*. New York: Continuum Press, 1982.

Lucy Evelyn Cheesman
(1881–1969)

England
Entomologist

Although some may consider entomology an odd passion, particularly for a woman, Evelyn Cheesman loved insects and devoted the majority of her life to collecting and preserving thousands of specimens. In the process she traveled to exotic locations, many of them previously unvisited by a Western woman.

Lucy Evelyn Cheesman was born in Westwall, Kent, in 1881 to a moderately well-to-do family. An early lover of nature and of animals, the young woman wanted to be a veterinarian, but the profession was closed to women in those days.

During World War I she accepted a civil service post as a typist, and after the war she was transferred to the Imperial College of Science Zoological Society. She was assigned to the Insect House in Regent's Park Zoo. After taking a course in entomology, Evelyn began making presentations to children's groups. She also wrote books for children about insects, occasionally attributing human characteristics to the flying and crawling creatures.

In 1923 Cheesman was asked to join a scientific research expedition to the Marquesa and Galapagos islands. Enthralled by the islands, the culture, and the vast array of insect specimens, she left the tour in Tahiti to undertake her own adventure. Relying on the natives for advice on which trails to take, Cheesman wandered across Madeira, Trinidad, and Martinique for months, collecting over five hundred specimens in the process. On returning to England, she gave up her job with the zoo to devote her life to collecting and writing.

Funded by the British Museum, Evelyn Cheesman traveled to the New Hebrides in 1928 and wandered into a sector populated by cannibals. Unknowingly, she had fortunately hired as her guide a young boy who was considered mad and a murderer; thus, the cannibals believed she possessed strong magic and did not harm her. They assumed she was collecting insects for some act of sorcery, and they honored her with a feast. The cannibals had never been visited by any westerner, man or woman, but Evelyn Cheesman gained their admiration. She stayed with them alone for over two years, observing their taboos and superstitions and treating them with respect.

Cheesman spent more than twelve years in the field, including one year in the interior of Dutch New Guinea, where she gathered over forty-two thousand specimens of parasitic worms, leeches, reptiles, and spiders. She funded the majority of the trips herself with the proceeds from her prolific writing, sixteen books in all, and financed eight solo expeditions to the southwest Pacific Islands. She rarely took supplies with her into the jungle and relied on what she could find or what was offered to her by the natives.

In 1939 Cheesman returned to the civil service as a censor and plane spotter. She also drew contour maps of the South Pacific Islands for the military. She was injured in a railway accident and developed arthritic complications, but after hip replacement surgery, she undertook her last expedition to the mountains of New Caledonia when she was over seventy.

References and Suggested Reading

Macksey, Joan, and Kenneth Macksey. *The Guinness Guide to Feminine Achievement*. Enfield, England: Guinness Superlatives, Ltd., 1975.

Robinson, Jane. *Wayward Women: A Guide to Women Travellers*. New York: Oxford University Press, 1990.

Eugenie Clark
(1922–   )

United States
Oceanographer/Ichthyologist

Courtesy of the Library of Congress

E ugenie Clark has been called "The Shark Lady" and "The Lady with a Spear," both mantles of honor for having done more than any other woman to bring the mysterious undersea world to the surface light. As an ichthyologist, she has studied species of fish and other sea creatures in almost every body of salt water on earth, including the Atlantic, the Pacific, the South Pacific, and the Red Sea. Even though she is diminutive in stature, she is not short on courage and is rarely intimidated by coming nose to nose with sharks or barracuda.

Eugenie Clark, who likes to be called Genie, was born in New York City. Her father, Charles, died when she was two, forcing her Japanese mother, Yumico Mitomi, to go to work to support the family. When Eugenie reached school age, her mother could not afford afternoon child care, even if it had been available in those days. Thus, the young girl was left to wander through the city's aquarium in Lower Manhattan while Yumico worked. At nine years old, Eugenie Clark felt right at home and safe among the fishes. When birthdays and Christmases rolled around, Genie begged for a fifteen-gallon aquarium and began collecting her own scaled creatures. Overtime the menagerie grew, with the addition of an alligator, a toad, and a snake.

As Genie observed her fish, both in her tank at home and during her afternoons at the aquarium, she realized, even then, that the fins and tail were used for turning and the strong body muscles were used for swimming. She later applied these techniques in her own underwater explorations. Both Eugenie Clark and her mother loved the water and spent much of their free time at the shore. Yumico was a strong swimmer and taught the young girl to put chewing gum in her ears to prevent water from entering the canal.

After high school Eugenie Clark enrolled at New York's Hunter College, majoring in zoology. Between classes she could be found in the laboratory "playing" with the fish, noting the particular characteristics of each variety. Her summers were spent at the University of Michigan Biological Station. After earning her degree in 1942 she worked as a chemist with Celanese Corporation, an unusual occupation for a woman in that decade. Clark attended graduate school at New York University, where she earned her master's degree in 1946 and her doctorate in 1950. Her doctoral study on artificial insemination and reproductive behavior became the basis for much of her later investigation, particularly with the Fish and Wildlife Service.

In 1947 she moved to La Jolla, California as a research assistant in animal behavior for the Scripps Institute of Oceanography. While there, she made her first dive in a helmet and her first dive with a face mask. She preferred the latter because the helmet was heavy and limited her mobility underwater. During those dives she had initial introductions to sharks, those creatures which would fascinate her and continue to be a focal point of her later studies.

Commissioned by the Fish and Wildlife Service in 1947, Eugenie had the opportunity to conduct independent research in the Phillippines as the only woman scientist on a project surveying animal behavior. En route, however, she was detained in Hawaii by the Federal Bureau of Investigation (FBI), who wanted to verify her credentials in light of her Japanese ancestry. Due to the extent of the delay, she was replaced on the expedition by a man. Later the same year she was invited to the Lerner Marine Lab in Bimini, West Indies, to analyze the vision mechanism in salt water fish. After those dives she returned to New York as a research assistant for the American Museum of Natural History.

In 1949, through the Office of Naval Research, she toured many of the South Sea Islands, including Koror, Kwajalein, Guam, Saipan, and Micronesia, to collect samples of poisonous fish. Tiring of corrupting tide pools to obtain samples, she went diving with some of the native fishermen. While underwater she watched as the fishermen lunged at their prey, spearing them neatly and securely, and she immediately saw the skill as a more effective method of retrieving samples. She asked for lessons, the fishermen obliged, and as with the rest of her growing talents, she was a quick study in spear fishing.

While diving she spotted a giant clam, measuring more than four feet across. Although the diver likely weighed less than the clam, Eugenie was determined to bring this one in and looped a line around the massive mollusk. She succeeded in moving it a few feet but had to release it when she realized it was entirely too large to pull all the way to the surface.

After being awarded a Fulbright Scholarship in 1950, Eugenie Clark undertook her master project. Working for the Ghardaqa Biological Station in Egypt and the Hebrew University at Elat, Israel, she examined the virtually unexplored recesses of the Red Sea. She was the first to study the sea since 1880 and the only woman scientist ever to conduct research there.

The Red Sea is one of the saltiest and least spoiled bodies of water on earth with many spots plunging thousands of feet below the surface. Consequently, the marine life playing in and out of the coral reefs and diving into the darkest depths is more diverse than in any other body of water. One of the species, known as sea cows, is over eleven feet long and could account for tales of sea monsters or myths of mermaids. Clark's primary focus during the study was on the sea anemone and the clown fish that live symbiotically among its tentacles, as well as the reproductive habits of pipefish, a unique species because it is the males that give birth. In addition, she continued to collect specimens for both the United States National Museum and the United States Navy.

While working in the area, she married Dr. Ilias Papakonstantinou, an orthopedic surgeon she met while in New York. He came to Cairo for the wedding and the couple honeymooned "in" the Red Sea. Returning to New York, Clark accepted a teaching post at Hunter College, her alma mater, and awaited her next aquatic assignment, which arrived in short order.

In 1955 Eugenie Clark was asked to set up the Cape Haze Marine Biological Lab in Sarasota, Florida. She became the lab's executive director, remaining there until 1967. The chief topic of experimentation in the lab was the behavior of sharks, and it was through her intimate, occasionally too intimate, contact with those denizens of the deep that she gained great respect from the scientific community, as well as the title "Shark Lady." Believing that sharks were capable of certain intelligence, Eugenie dedicated herself to seeking scientific proof. Using a Skinnerian method of training, she taught the creatures that response equals reward. The sharks learned to push an object with their nose and then swim away, whereupon they were rewarded with morsels of food.

Clark accepted a teaching position in the Department of Biology at the University of Maryland in 1968. Continuing to do work in the field, she made three trips to the Yucatan Peninsula in the early 1970s, underwritten by the National Geographic Society, to study an unusual specimen known as the "sleeping" shark. The sharks were virtually immobile and appeared to have lost their predatory instincts. After making ninety-nine dives Eugenie Clark confirmed her theory that the area where the sharks were "sleeping" contained a certain amount of fresh water as well as salt water. Concluding that an influx of fresh water into a shark's habitat would produce a more passive creature was a scientific breakthrough in shark research.

Although retired from her full-time teaching post, Clark maintains her position as senior research scientist at the university. She also teaches a class each fall on sea monsters and deep sea sharks.

Eugenie Clark has received numerous awards, including three honorary doctorates, commendations from the National Geographic Society and the Explorers Club, and the Gold Medal from the Society of Women Geographers. She is the author of three books, including *Lady with a Spear* (1953), which was a Book-of-the-Month-Club selection and translated into eight languages as well as braille. Other works include *The Lady and the Sharks* (1969), *The Desert beneath the Sea* (with Ann McGovern) (1991), and over one hundred sixty-five articles for scientific journals and popular magazines. She has lectured at over seventy colleges and universities in the United States and in twenty-one foreign countries.

In addition, Clark has been consultant, narrator, co-director, or principal in twenty-four half- and one-hour television specials in the United States and foreign countries. "The Sharks," a National Geographic Special in 1982, holds the highest Nielsen rating for the Public Broadcasting System (PBS). Clark also aided in the creation of the first IMAX film, "Great Sharks," which debuted in May of 1993.

With all of these accomplishments and honors to her credit, Eugenie Clark cites two instances as her favorite memories. The first was her time at the Red Sea, an area for which she holds a romantic fascination. The other was a night she spent among sea lions in Australia. Borrowing blankets from her hotel, she disguised herself as a female sea lion, waded out to join the creatures, and was accepted into their fold for a restful sleep under the stars.

References and Suggested Reading

Butts, Ellen, and Joyce Schwartz. *Eugenie Clark: Adventures of a Shark Scientist.* North Haven, CT: Linnet Books, 2000.

Emberlin, D. *Contributions of Women in Science.* New York: Dillon Press, 1977.

Facklam, Margery. *Wild Animals, Gentle Women.* New York: Harcourt Brace Jovanovich, 1978.

McGovern, Ann. *Shark Lady: True Adventures of Eugenie Clark.* New York: Four Winds Press, 1979.

Geraldyn "Jerrie" Cobb
(1931–   )

United States
Aviator/Humanitarian

Courtesy of the Library of Congress

Although she was one of the first women to satisfy the criteria of the National Aeronautic and Space Administration (NASA) to become an astronaut, Jerrie Cobb has never flown in space. Due to circumstances beyond her control, the program was suspended but, decades later, she has not surrendered her dream of travel among the stars.

Geraldyn "Jerrie" Cobb was born in Norman, Oklahoma, in 1931. Her father, Lieutenant Colonel William Harvey Cobb, was a career Army officer; consequently, the young girl and her mother, Helena Butler Stone, spent their lives being shuttled from base to base. Jerrie was educated in the base schools but often escaped the regimented life by horseback riding, usually bareback.

When she was twelve years old, however, she gave up horses for a new passion. In an attempt to get a commission into the Army Air Corps, William Cobb learned to fly. One afternoon he surprised his young daughter by inviting her to come along and thus began her long love of flying. William did not get the appointment but Jerrie was hooked. She worked at a local horse ranch, waxed airplanes, and took whatever odd jobs she could find to pay for flying lessons. By 1947 she had soloed and qualified for a pilot's license.

In 1948 Jerrie Cobb entered the Oklahoma College for Women in Chickasha, but classrooms were too confining for her. She left after one year to resume the lessons she considered more important. By her eighteenth birthday she had acquired both her commercial pilot's license and her flight instructor's license.

Earthbound for a short while, Jerrie played semiprofessional softball for the Oklahoma City Queens, saving as much of her income as possible. When there was enough money, she purchased a World War II surplus plane and by 1951 was ready to hire out as a charter pilot. Jobs came slowly and although she did not encounter blatant prejudice, it seemed clients preferred male pilots.

In 1952 she received an offer from Jack Ford, a former Air Force pilot and owner of Fleetway, Incorporated. Fleetway contracted pilots to deliver surplus military planes to American allies in Europe and around the world. In that capacity Cobb became the only woman in the United States who served as an international ferry pilot, flying B–17s, T–6Gs, and other aircraft across the ocean. Eventually she was appointed chief pilot and supervisor of all South American operations. The routes were often difficult and some of the aircraft were not well equipped. While on one flight, she had engine trouble and had to make a forced landing in Colombia on a narrow strip wedged between the ocean and the Andes. On another, she was arrested in Ecuador as a Peruvian spy because the plane she was ferrying had Peruvian markings.

The job offered more than financial security and prestige, however. On a trip to Jamaica, Jack Ford proposed marriage and Jerrie accepted. They had been engaged for two years before a plane he was taxiing for take-off exploded, killing him instantly. Devastated, Jerrie returned to Oklahoma where she flew as a test pilot for Aero Design and Engineering Company. In 1956 she established several world records, including the first nonstop flight from Guatemala to Oklahoma City and an altitude record of 30,361 feet.

In 1960 her teenage fantasies were realized when she was invited to undergo a battery of eighty-seven tests to qualify for NASA astronaut training. NASA brought a select group to one of their testing facilities to explore the theory that women might be better equipped than men both physiologically and psychologically for travel in space. Among the thirteen women, called "Astronettes," to qualify for the Mercury 13 Project, Jerrie Cobb was the front runner, placing in the top 1 to 2 percent of both women and men in ability to adjust.

At the time of the NASA trials, she had logged over ten thousand hours of flight time in every type of aircraft but one, and it was that one which eventually scrapped the women's astronaut program for several years. Experts, including John Glenn, testified before Congress that astronauts, both men and women, should also be jet pilots. At that time no woman had ever flown a jet. In 1962 Jerrie Cobb pleaded the case before Congress but the decision stood.

With two major disappointments in her life, Cobb decided to make a drastic change, and in the process, to make the world a better place. In 1963 she left the United States for Colombia, South America, where she pledged her time as a bush pilot, running supplies from the Catholic mission to the indigenous peoples along the Amazon. For thirty-five years she flew antibiotics, food and clothing, and doctors to Brazil, Colombia, Bolivia, Peru, Venezuela, and Ecuador, where she served over six million people. For her selfless service, she received a nomination for the Nobel Peace Prize.

In 1969 she danced on the wings of her plane under the moonlight when she heard of Neil Armstrong's giant leap for mankind. According to her autobiography, *Solo Pilot* (1997), the Amazonian villagers of Colombia were not terribly impressed with Armstrong's accomplishment, for their shamans "flew to the moon all the time."

Returning to the United States after three and a half decades, Cobb was surprised and pleased to discover a grassroots movement underway to restore her right to fly into space. Ironically, that event could be made possible by John Glenn's return to NASA to test the effects of space travel on aging men. If a man, why not a woman?

References and Suggested Reading

Dunn, Marcia. "NASA Pioneer Asks for Her Shot at Space." *Washington Post*, 13 July 1998: A6.
Jerrie Cobb Foundation Web site. *http://www.jerrie-cobb.org/*
NASA Web site. *http://www.quest.arc.nasa.gov/women/*
"Stargazer." *People Weekly*, 19 October 1998, 50: 66.

Jacqueline Cochran
(c. 1910–1980)

United States
Aviator

Courtesy of the Library of Congress

A true rags-to-riches tale, flyer and businesswoman Jacqueline Cochran rose from abject poverty and an early career as a beautician to become an icon in aviation history, the director of the Women's Airforce Service Pilots (WASPS), and the head of a successful cosmetics firm. She holds more awards, records, and firsts, including being the first to break the sound barrier, than perhaps any other woman aviator.

Jacqueline Cochran was born in Pensacola, Florida, but having been orphaned in infancy, she was unaware of her actual date of birth. Taken in by a poor family, she grew up in the sawmill camps of southern Georgia and northern Florida. Funds were so minimal that she often had to catch fish in order to eat for the day; consequently, she acquired a strong work ethic early in life, babysitting for pennies when she was only a child herself. At eight years old, Jacqueline quit school and went to work in the cotton mills of Columbus, Georgia. Working twelve-hour shifts for six cents an hour, she eventually saved enough money to take classes at a local beauty school.

As a hairdresser Cochran jumped from shop to shop, relocating in Alabama, Florida, Pennsylvania, and finally landing in New York City. While working in the Saks Fifth Avenue beauty salon, she met banker/industrialist Floyd Bostwick Odlum, an aviator who held world records for both jet and reciprocating aircraft flights. Jacqueline listened wistfully to his stories of soaring into the skies and knew she had to follow.

In 1932 she spent her vacation taking flying lessons at Roosevelt Field on Long Island. After only three days of instruction, she took the plane up by herself, and in less than three weeks she rented a craft and flew to Montreal. Quitting her job, she relocated to San Diego, California, and enrolled in flight school but was frustrated by having to wait her turn among the other students. She bought an old plane for twelve hundred dollars and convinced an air officer friend to teach her the finer points of flight.

By 1934 she had earned her pilot's license and floated up, over thirty thousand meters, in a biplane with canvas wings. The unheated, unpressurized cockpit forced Cochran to inhale oxygen through a tube. When she reached the highest altitude, the oxygen tube burst, but she managed to land the plane quickly before oxygen deprivation caused serious physical damage. In the same year she was the only American woman entered in the McRobertson London to Melbourne air race, but mechanical problems caused her to ditch the plane in flight.

To support her flying, in 1934 Cochran founded a cosmetics firm bearing her name. Whether it was a quality line or whether the product sold merely through name recognition, the firm garnered millions of dollars annually. She was known to land her plane, taxi to the end of the runway, and carefully reapply her makeup and comb her hair before climbing down from the cockpit. She was twice named Woman of the Year in Business by an Associated Press poll of newspaper editors.

Cochran was the first and only woman to enter the trans-American Bendix Race in 1935. Reentering that competition annually, she placed third in 1937 and won the coveted trophy in an untried Seversky fighter plane in 1938. By that time she had married her inspiration and mentor, Floyd Odlum, then the owner and operator of a six-hundred-acre ranch in California.

During World War II Jacqueline Cochran piloted a bomber to England, the first woman to fly a war plane across the Atlantic. There she joined the British Air Transport Auxiliary as a flight captain and trained other women pilots for war transport service. She headed the same type of training program for the Army Air Forces after returning to the United States and in 1943 was named director of the Women's Airforce Service Pilots or WASPS. Over twenty-five thousand women applied for the program but only one thousand fulfilled the strenuous requirements to graduate and become auxiliary pilots for the war effort. Three decades later Jacqueline Cochran successfully lobbied Congress for retirement benefits for those women.

Near the end of the war, Cochran was pegged as Pacific and European correspondent for *Liberty Magazine*. In that capacity, she reported on the Japanese surrender, met Mao Tse-tung, interviewed Madame Chiang Kai-shek, and covered the Nazi war crimes trials in Nuremberg. In 1945, she was the first woman civilian to be awarded the Distinguished Service Medal and was subsequently commissioned as a lieutenant colonel in both the Air Force Reserves and the Civil Air Patrol.

Continuing to venture where no woman had gone before, Jacqueline Cochran was the first to break the sound barrier in 1953, traveling at 625.5 miles per hour and joining the previously male-dominated "supersonic club." In addition, she served as the first woman president of the Fédération Aéronautique Internationale in 1959 and was the first to fly at Mach 2, twice the speed of sound, in 1960. Also in that year she became the first woman to land on an aircraft carrier, the USS *Independence*, which she did successfully, but after touching down the plane skidded off the wet surface of the ship and into the ocean. Both aviator and plane were fine, although Cochran was somewhat embarrassed. Two years later she piloted a jet across the Atlantic, yet another first for women, and in 1964 she logged a record-setting speed of 1,429 miles per hour.

Cochran was awarded the Harmon International Aviation Awards

Committee trophy six times as the most distinguished Aviator of the Year, and in 1950 was named Aviatrix of the Decade by that group. She held honorary doctorates from Russell Sage College and from Elmira College, where she was elected Woman of the Year in 1954. Honorary wings from the French, Chinese, Turkish, Spanish and Thailand Air Forces graced her portfolio, and for awhile she was a director of Northeast Airlines. She served on the boards of the African Research Foundation, the Air Force Academy Foundation, and the Camp Fire Girls. In 1977 she became the only living woman inducted into the American Aviation Hall of Fame.

Always intrigued by politics, Cochran was a strong supporter of and campaigner for Dwight David Eisenhower and sought her own congressional seat in California. She lost by a slim margin. In 1996, sixteen years after her death in Indio, California, Jacqueline Cochran garnered a posthumous honor when the United States Postal Service issued a fifty-cent international postcard stamp bearing a 1938 photograph of this stellar navigator of the skies.

References and Suggested Reading

Cochran, Jacqueline. *The Stars at Noon*. New York: Little, 1954.
"Jacqueline Cochran Flies into Philatelic History." *Stamps*, 30 March 1996, 255: 3.
Uglow, Jennifer S. *The International Dictionary of Women's Biography*. New York: Continuum Press, 1982.

Elizabeth "Bessie" Coleman (1892–1926)

United States
Aviator

Courtesy of the Library of Congress

Although she died before achieving her dream of founding a flight school, Bessie Coleman singlehandedly secured a place for African American aviators. She was the first black pilot in the United States and the first person of either gender or any race to earn an international license allowing her to fly anywhere in the world.

Elizabeth "Bessie" Coleman was born in 1892 in Atlanta, Texas, the twelfth of thirteen children. Her father, George, was a Native American day laborer and her mother, Susan, an African American domestic and farm worker. When Bessie was an infant, they moved to Waxahachie, Texas, and shortly afterward, George deserted his family to return to reservation lands in Oklahoma. Possessed of an indomitable spirit, Susan Coleman encouraged her children to improve their lot in life and insisted on their attending school. Bessie became an early and avid reader and the family bookkeeper. After working through high school, picking cotton and taking in laundry and ironing, she paid her way through one semester, all she could afford, at Langston Independent College in Oklahoma.

In 1912 Bessie moved to Chicago with her brothers and enrolled in Burnham's School of Beauty Culture. She was hired as a manicurist at the White Sox Barber Shop at Kominsky Park, and to supplement that salary, she ran a chili parlor down the street from the ball park.

Inspired by stories of other women aviators like Harriet Quimby, Bessie Coleman developed an interest in flying in 1917. She applied to several flight schools but was refused admission due to her ethnicity and gender. Rumors of her pursuit of a pilot's license were passed along to African American philanthropist Robert Abbott, the publisher of the *Chicago Defender*, a newspaper dedicated to black interests. After meeting the young woman Abbott suggested that she might find a more receptive training program in Europe. She studied French and departed for France in 1920, funded in part by monies raised by Abbott.

In France Coleman was admitted to the Caudron Aircraft Manufacturing Company training program in LeCrotoy and later in Paris. She received her pilot's license in 1921, the first awarded to an American woman by the French Fédération Aéronautique Internationale. In addition she was the only person in the world, of either gender, to be granted an international pilot's license, permitting her to fly anywhere on the globe. At the time, she was the sole African American pilot in the world.

Returning to the United States in 1922, she encountered the same prejudices she had left behind, prejudices that were a product of the Jim Crow laws in force at the time. The only avenue open to her in her new profession was barnstorming, acrobatic feats and daredevil stunts performed for crowds of spectators on the ground. On Labor Day, 1922, Coleman performed daring dives and rolls at Curtiss Field in Garden City, New York. Because the show was the initial public flight undertaken by a black woman in the United States, reporters surged to the area, and Coleman was featured in a series of newsreel films.

After her second outing at the Checkerboard Airdome in Chicago, she decided to use her fee to purchase three Army surplus Curtiss biplanes with the hope of saving her purses from future shows to found a flight school for African American pilots, both women and men. At her third exhibition she met David Behnecke, the founder of the International Airline Pilots Association, who became her manager. During that presentation, she successfully made a record-breaking parachute jump after the woman who had been scheduled to do so backed out.

In 1923, during her first demonstration on the West Coast, on a flight from Santa Monica to Los Angeles, her aircraft's engine stalled, plummeting the plane three hundred feet to the ground. The machine was completely destroyed and Coleman had to be cut out of the wreckage. Throughout an extensive recuperation, she lectured on flight in various cities. By 1924 she was off the ground once again, pulling aerial advertisements in her trademark cap, goggles, white shirt, tie, and boots.

Hired by the Negro Welfare League of Jacksonville, Florida, Coleman was scheduled as part of the First of May celebration in Orlando in 1926. However, when she was told by the organizers that blacks would not be allowed to attend the event, she refused to fly. The presenters reneged, and aviators were sent up to drop leaflets on the African American communities, inviting them to attend the celebration.

By then dubbed "Queen Bess," she paid to lease a plane for the Florida performance but her white mechanic, William D. Willis, had ferried the craft from Texas since blacks were not allowed to rent aircraft. The rental had encountered mechanical problems between Texas and Florida; thus, Willis and Coleman thought it best to take the plane up on a practice run on April 30. With Willis piloting, the craft had been in the air for twelve minutes, climbing to an altitude of three thousand feet. The mechanic attempted a nose dive but could not get the plane to pull up. Although safety had always been foremost in her mind, Bessie Coleman was not wearing a seat belt or parachute. She was thrown from the plane, two thousand feet above the ground at approximately 110 miles per hour. The airplane continued to spiral downward and crashed nose first, killing Willis as well.

Although she did not live to see her ambition fulfilled, the Bessie Coleman Flight School was opened in Los Angeles in 1929, followed by the Bessie Coleman Aero Clubs, and the periodical, *The Bessie Coleman Aero News* in 1930. In 1931 the Coleman Aero Club sponsored the first all-black air show in the United States. Each Memorial Day a squadron of African American aviators fly over her grave in Chicago and drop bouquets of flowers to honor this woman who was an early champion for equality by refusing to perform for a segregated audience decades before the civil rights movement. This act of courage might be equated to that of Rosa Parks in Birmingham years later.

References and Suggested Reading

Creasman, Kim. "Black Birds in the Sky: The Legacies of Bessie Coleman and Dr. Mae Jemison." *The Journal of Negro History* (Winter 1997) 82: 158–169.

Freydberg, Elizabeth Hadley. *Bessie Coleman: The Brownskin Lady Bird*. New York: Garland, 1994.

Malveaux, Julianne. "Stepping Out into the Unknown: Bessie Coleman and the Millennium." *Black Issues in Higher Education*, 17 February 2000, 16: 34.

Rich, Doris L. *Queen Bess: Daredevil Aviator*. Washington, DC: Smithsonian Institution Press, 1993.

Eileen Marie Collins
(1956–   )

United States
Astronaut

T he first woman to command a space shuttle, Eileen Collins is a study in perseverance. Despite the financial turmoil of her youth and the obvious pressures of competing in a man's world, she achieved her dream through hard work and with much grace.

Eileen Marie Collins was born in Elmira, New York, in 1956. Her father, James, was a postal worker who took his children on family picnics to nearby Harris Hill, the site of the National Soaring Museum. At seven years of age Eileen's fascination with flight was born watching gliders soar above the family as they ate their lunch on the ground. Thus inspired, she began to devour stories about famous women pilots, including Amelia Earhart and Jacqueline Cochran.

James and Rose Marie Collins separated when Eileen was nine. Since their Catholic upbringing would not allow them to divorce, maintaining separate households put enormous financial strain on the family. By working in a catalog showroom, Eileen Collins saved enough money to earn an associate's degree from Corning Community College. While taking classes, she served pizza in the evenings to pay for flying lessons. She soloed and earned her wings at age twenty. Combining her desire for both an education and flight, she entered Syracuse University on an Air Force ROTC scholarship and was graduated in 1978 with a degree in mathematics and science. Eventually, she was awarded master's degrees from Stanford University in science and from Webster University in St. Louis, Missouri, in space systems management.

Honoring her commitment to the Air Force, Collins went on active duty in 1978, undertaking a year of pilot training at Vance Air Force Base in Oklahoma. She was one of only four women in a class of three hundred twenty. Transferred to Travis Air Force base in California, she met Pat Youngs, a fellow flight instructor and the man she was to marry. While at Travis, Collins flew twenty-six different types of planes in one year, some of which were going up for the first time with her as solo pilot. In 1989 she became only the second woman admitted to the Air Force's test pilot school. Intermittently, between 1986 and 1989, she served as assistant professor of mathematics and T-41 flight instructor at the United States Air Force Academy in Colorado.

In 1990 Collins was selected from a field of thirteen by the National Aeronautics and Space Administration (NASA) as the first woman to participate in shuttle pilot training. Five years later she was at the helm of the space shuttle *Discovery* for its first rendezvous with the Russian space station *Mir*. After that voyage Collins was grounded for nine months when it was discovered she was pregnant with her daughter,

Bridget. By 1997, however, she was back in space, aboard the shuttle to bring fellow astronaut, Jerry Linenger, home from his tour on *Mir*.

Colonel Collins was awarded ultimate recognition in 1998 when she was selected to command the shuttle *Columbia* on a mission to launch the largest X-ray telescope ever flown into space. Called the Chandra for Nobel Prize winning astrophysicist, Subrahmanyan Chandrasekhar, the telescope had been nearly twenty years in development, was forty-feet long, and weighed over fifty thousand pounds. A sister to the Hubble telescope earlier placed in orbit, Chandra was the second of four observatories planned by NASA. The 4.3 billion dollar mission was delayed twice due to mechanical problems, including a leak in the fuel tank, but finally jettisoned into the night sky at eight thousand miles per hour, making Eileen Collins the first woman shuttle commander in history.

Collins was awarded the Air Force Meritorious Service Medal, the Armed Forces Expeditionary Medal for service in Grenada, and the NASA Space Flight Medal. Over her career she logged over five thousand hours of flight time in thirty different types of aircraft, including four hundred nineteen hours in space. During a White House reception, after being named shuttle commander, she said, "It is my hope that all children, boys and girls, will see this mission [*Columbia*] and be inspired to reach for their dreams, because dreams do come true." For Eileen Collins, they certainly have as she traversed the distance between watching gliders on a summer hillside to gliding among the stars.

References and Suggested Reading

Aviation Archives Web site. *http://www.womeninaviation.com*

"Collins and Columbia Launch Chandra." *Sky and Telescope* (October 1999) 98: 16.

Frazier, Allison. "Colonel Eileen Collins in Washington." *Ad Astra* (November/ December 1999) 11: 7.

"Going Where No Woman Has Gone Before." *Christian Science Monitor* 19 July 1999, 1.

Sheridan, David. "An American First: Eileen Collins." *NEA Today*, 15 September 95, 14: 7.

Sherr, Lynn. "A Commanding Position." *Ms. Magazine* (July/August 1998) 9: 23.

Alexandra David-Neel
(1868–1969)

→

France

Asia Explorer

From the age of five, when she first ran away from home, Alexandra David-Neel possessed a rebellious spirit and an unorthodox view of life. She spent the majority of her adult years wandering through Central Asia and was the first European woman to view the sacred and forbidden city of Lhasa in Tibet.

Alexandra David-Neel was born in 1868 in Sainte-Monde, France, the only child of Louis Pierre and Alexandrine Borghmans David. Her mother's dream was to have a son who would enter the service of the church, and she often failed to hide her disappointment in the young girl. Feeling unwanted, Alexandra escaped first into a world of fantasy and then into the real world. At the age of five she ran away and hid in the Vincennes Wood, only to be retrieved by the local constabulary.

Her parents, feeling the child needed stricter discipline to control her independence, placed her in a Calvinist convent. At the convent school Alexandra buried herself in the library, consuming all she could find on Eastern religions and mysticism, particularly Tibetan philosophy. When she was fifteen, she wrapped her possessions in a sheet and departed the convent for Britain; two years later she left Britain for Italy, crossing Saint Gothard pass on foot.

Returning to Paris, she enrolled in the Sorbonne. Although she was still enamored of Hindu philosophy and mired in research, she was also critical of her times. She wrote a feminist text, drew up a declaration of rights for women, and demanded a salary for housewives. In 1891, tiring of the Sorbonne, she set sail for Ceylon on an eighteen-month journey. She reached the border of Sikkim but had to turn back due to a shortage of funds.

Again in France, Alexandra turned to the theater. Using the stage name of Mademoiselle Myrial, she embarked on a singing career although she had no formal training. While making the rounds of small venues, she was offered the position of lead singer with the Hanoi Opera, which she gladly accepted and maintained for two years. In 1897 she left Hanoi for the Athens Opera and traveled to Tunis where she met Philippe-Francois Neel, a dashing railroad engineer. They were married in 1904, on his condition that she give up the theater and on her condition that she continue to travel. The marriage lasted until his death, although the couple never lived together.

Holding Philippe to his premarital promise to finance her excursions, Alexandra departed for what was to be a twelve-month trek to India that turned into fourteen years. At last in a place where she could study the original texts, she returned to her contemplation of Buddhism. She met with wise men, begged for translations, meditated, and eventually adopted the Buddhist religion. The pinnacle of her soul's journey was an interview with the Dalai Lama while he was in exile in Bhutan.

In 1910 David-Neel was contacted by the French Ministry of Education to conduct Oriental research in India and Burma. For her service she was made a knight of honor and received the Gold Medal from the Paris Geographical Society. During the same period, she lived as an ascetic hermit in a cave near Sikkim, thirteen thousand feet above sea level. Her only nod to civilization was the rugs she placed on the cave floor as she recreated the contemplative life of Buddhist nuns. She discovered the art of "tumo," mentally controlling her body's temperature to keep from freezing in the chilled altitude.

Although slowly bankrupting her husband, Alexandra traveled in Burma, Japan, and China, arriving in 1918 at the monastery of Kumbum. There she settled for two years, undertaking the translation of a host of Tibetan texts. By 1922 she was off again, wandering in the Gobi Desert.

Distressed that with all her devoted study she was still denied access to the holy city of Lhasa, David-Neel became obsessed with going there. At age fifty-five she disguised herself as a beggar, darkened her face with cocoa and charcoal, braided yak hair into her own, pretended to be simple-minded, and set off in search of her Holy Grail. She traveled with only one companion, Lama Anphur Yongden, a young Indian boy from Sikkim, whom she later adopted. Assuming the role of the old Tibetan mother of the young boy, Alexandra trudged through rain, mud, and snow and over mountain passes higher than eighteen thousand feet in the dead of winter. Carrying only the minimum supplies, the two traveled at night, skirting robbers and officials, and slept out of doors during the day. After four months Alexandra David-Neel penetrated the city of Lhasa, the first European woman to do so. She stayed two months before being discovered and told to depart.

Returning to France in 1924, she was hailed as a national hero and considered an authority on Tibet and Tibetan Buddhism. She became a prolific writer, composing nine works on Oriental mysticism, her philosophy, and her travels. The autobiographical *My Journey to Lhasa* (1930) and *The Power of Nothingness* sold well and initiated a revitalized European interest in Asia. Most of her books were reissued in paperback during the last three decades of the twentieth century and most are still in print.

She went back to China in 1936, living on the Tibetan frontier for six years. She and her adopted son settled in the Alps when she was in her eighties. On her one hundredth birthday, however, she renewed her passport to be ready for any adventures that might yet come her way.

References and Suggested Reading

David-Neel, Alexandra. *My Journey to Lhasa*. New York: Harper's, 1927.

Foster, Barbara, and Michael Foster. *Forbidden Journey*. New York: Overlook Press, 1997.

Foster, Barbara, Michael Foster, and Lawrence Durrell. *The Secret Lives of Alexandra David-Neel: A Biography of the Explorer of Tibet and Its Hidden Practices*. New York: Overlook Press, 1998.

Meta Ann "Annie" Doak Dillard
(1945–   )

United States
Naturalist

H ailed as a mystic and religious writer by some and a naturalist by others, author Annie Dillard has done more to reconnect humans and nature than any wordsmith since Henry David Thoreau. Although most of her exploration has been introspective, she has awakened others to the wonders of the natural world and the simple pleasures of observation.

Meta Ann "Annie" Doak Dillard was born in Pittsburgh, Pennsylvania, in 1945. Although she was raised in the luxury afforded by old money—her great-great grandfather founded the company that became American Standard—Annie had little appreciation for the lethargy produced by wealth. Her father, Frank Doak, floated from job to job, finally becoming a voice in radio commercials; her mother, Pam Lambert Doak, Dillard characterized as "completely irrepressible." The money permitted the young woman a private school education.

Needing to put distance between herself and her idiosyncratic family, Annie Dillard enrolled in Hollins College in Virginia at age seventeen. Her professor of creative writing, R. H. W. Dillard, became her mentor and then her husband. The two were married at the end of her sophomore year. In 1967 she earned a bachelor's degree and a master's in English one year later.

After her course work was completed, Dillard invested several years in the contemplative life, painting and reading exhaustively. She maintained a reading journal, noting thoughts of others, coupled with her own observations on the natural world. In 1971 a near fatal case of pneumonia created the desire to live her own life, rather than doing so vicariously through others. She left her library and went camping.

While wending her way through the Virginia valleys, Dillard noted the minute in nature, the interplay between the tiniest of creatures, and the perfection of the most fragile blossoms. These meditations inspired *Pilgrim at Tinker Creek* (1974), a work that catapulted the young woman out of her reverie and into the international arena. Written as narratives, the essays took the form of small dramas in which every blade of grass and each quivering leaf played a role. The work became a best-seller, inspiring multitudes to abandon their hurly burly workaday worlds and seek inspiration from natural vistas. Dillard was shocked at the reaction. "I thought forty monks would read it," she uttered.

When *Pilgrim at Tinker Creek* was awarded the Pulitzer Prize in 1975, Annie Dillard was unprepared for the limelight and the hordes beating their way to her doorstep. Her marriage was coming to an end, and there was really nothing holding her in Virginia. Needing to get away, she accepted a position as scholar-in-residence at Western Washington University in Bellingham, where she taught from 1975 to 1978.

In Washington she met Gary Clevidence, an anthropology professor at Fairhaven College. They moved together to Middletown, Connecticut, in 1979 and were married in 1980. Dillard taught at Wesleyan University during the school year and spent her summers on Cape Cod, where she could observe, write, and care for her infant daughter. The couple separated in 1987.

Since the beginning of her writing career, critics had compared Dillard to Thoreau; consequently, she read everything she could find about the naturalist. A new biography of Thoreau by author Bob Richardson appeared, and as Annie read it, she had an overwhelming desire to meet the writer. Although she had never done so before, she penned a fan letter to Richardson, suggesting that she would like to meet him. Richardson agreed, and shortly after their first meeting, he became her third husband.

With several collections of essays, one novel, various articles, and volumes of poetry to her credit, Annie Dillard prefers the quiet life. Her desire for something more, ingrained from her childhood, led to her conversion to Catholicism in her twenties, and religious philosophy permeates her work. She spends much of her free time in Benedictine monasteries, taking part in the daily rigors of that life, and serves in a soup kitchen. Although most of her excursions have been trips of the soul, she has, like Thoreau, inspired many of her readers to appreciate nature and its nuances.

References and Suggested Reading

Dillard, Annie. *An American Childhood*. New York: HarperCollins, 1998.
Lander, Cheryl. "EarthSaint: Annie Dillard." *Earthlight Magazine* (Winter 1997) 24: 1–4.

Florence Catherine Douglas Dixie
(1855–1905)

England
Journalist/Activist

One of the most widely read of the lady Victorian travelers, Florence Dixie, though born to royalty, had an affinity for the common man and an activist spirit concerning human rights. She explored extensively in the remote southernmost regions of South America and reported on the war-ravaged continent of Africa.

Florence Catherine Douglas Dixie was born in 1857 in London. Her father, Archibald William Douglas, was the Marquis of Queensberry. In 1860 Douglas was cleaning his gun, which accidentally fired, fatally wounding him. Florence's mother, Caroline Margaret Clayton Douglas, took the young girl and her twin brother, James, and moved to France. Over the next few years the family relocated from city to city, instilling a love for travel in Florence but doing little for her formal schooling. At eighteen she met and married Sir Alexander Beaumont Dixie.

Because her family could easily afford to travel, Florence Dixie persuaded her husband, her brother, and other close family friends to accompany her on an outing. The site she choose was Patagonia, an infrequently traveled desert region at the southern tip of South America. It was probably the dearth of information about the area that figured in her selection, and her response to those who queried her choice of destination was usually, "Because it is there." Once they arrived on the strip between the Andes and the Atlantic, the Dixies procured fifty horses and three mules for their foray. Florence was a fearless horsewoman, often leaping on the bare back of her mount.

The party planned to hunt for food, but game in the region was in short supply, although they did down an ostrich, a yellow puma, and an ibis, from which they made soup. Arriving in the village of the Tehuelche Indians, the Dixies traded some of their provisions for meat. The Indians seemed particularly intrigued by Florence for she was likely the first Western woman they had ever seen.

One peaceful morning Florence had just awakened to a crisp blue sky when she heard a rumbling like thunder that stirred everyone in the camp. The ground trembled and groaned and the dirt and rock undulated. In disbelief she realized they were in the midst of an earthquake. When the tremor had passed, fortunately with little damage to persons or possessions, the native guides were more astonished than anyone, stating there had never been an earthquake in Patagonia before. In addition to the earthquake, the Dixie party survived a prairie fire, incessant rains, and voracious mosquitos in their trek across the region.

Once back in Europe, Florence compiled her travel journals and published *Across Patagonia* in 1880. The book sold enough copies to secure her place as a travel author and to elicit an offer to be a correspondent from the *London Morning Post*. Although some questioned the *Post*'s choice of a correspondent and others hinted at favoritism to the peerage, Lady Dixie became a reporter assigned to cover the Boer War in Africa. The Boers were Dutch who were warring with the British over territory in South Africa, an area indigenous to the Zulus. Florence Dixie sided with the Zulus, feeling they were more entitled to their ancestral lands than either of the outside parties. Using her influence, she lobbied to have Cetawayo, King of Zululand, released from captivity and returned to power. Her mission was successful and although his reign was short-lived, Cetawayo was freed from British captivity in 1883.

Although she was not a trained sociologist, Florence Dixie was an effective activist. Her next cause was the plight of the Irish, for whom she raised money. It was her belief that they were the victims of British exploitation and deserving of aid. When an attack of rheumatic gout curtailed her travels in the mid-1880s, she turned to causes closer to home, advocating gender equality and women's rights, including the right to "rational dress," by which she meant slacks. She also wrote articles against vivisection and opposing hunting for sport, unusual for someone of the nobility. She died in 1905 of diphtheria.

References and Suggested Reading

Dixie, Florence. *Across Patagonia*. Online. 1998. University Electronic Text Research Center. University of Minnesota, Minneapolis. *http://etrc.lib.umn.edu/*

Stevenson, Catherine. *Victorian Women Travel Writers in Africa*. Boston: Twayne Publishers, 1982.

University of Southern Maine Web site. *http://www.usm.maine.edu*

Amelia Earhart
(1898–1937)

United States
Aviator

I n her time pioneering aviator Amelia Earhart was the most famous woman in the world, and decades after her mysterious disappearance her name is still universally recognized. Not only did she rapidly accumulate a series of firsts for her gender, she became a role model and an activist for women, opening the field of aviation and proving that stamina was not particular to men.

Amelia Earhart was born in 1898 in Atchison, Kansas. Her father, Edwin, an attorney for the railroad, and her mother, Amy, the first woman to climb Pike's Peak, gave their daughters unlimited freedom and shocked the neighborhood by allowing Amelia and her sister to wear bloomers and play with footballs and guns. The family moved often due to Edwin Earhart's bouts with alcoholism and the decline in the family's resources.

After graduating from high school in Chicago, Amelia planned to matriculate at Bryn Mawr, but a visit to Canada in 1917 altered her plans. She toured the Spadina Military Hospital, where the wounded of World War I had been transported, and she felt obligated to help. Taking a concentrated first-aid course from the Canadian Red Cross, she spent the balance of the war years as a volunteer nurse's aide. She worked in the dispensary, made beds, and delivered meals.

Inspired by her time at the hospital, she enrolled at Columbia University in 1919 in the premedical program, but by the end of her first year, she realized that medicine was not to be her career. Earhart dropped out of school and rejoined her parents, who at that time were living in Los Angeles. While in California, Amelia attended an air show in Long Beach. Although the show was primarily stunt flying, rolls, and dives for spectators, the young woman was transfixed. Her parents disapproved of her plans, probably for the first time in her life, but Amelia took a series of jobs, including working in the telephone company, to pay for flying lessons from a woman instructor, Neta Snook, who became her friend. She earned her pilot's license, bought her first plane, and performed in a few local meets, setting a women's altitude record of fourteen thousand feet in 1922.

When her parents' rocky marriage dissolved in 1924, Earhart moved back East to Boston and accepted a position in social work with immigrants at the Denison Settlement House. That was where she was when she received an invitation to join pilots Wilmer Stultz and Louis Gordon as a passenger and log keeper for a flight across the Atlantic. Although she would not be navigating the plane, the *Friendship*, she would be the first woman ever to cross the ocean by air. The three fliers kept their plans secret to avoid publicity and competition. The lack of media attention was short-lived, however, for the moment the plane landed, in Bunny Port, Wales, the pilots became international celebrities. Likely because of her gender, Earhart garnered most of the attention, which she found embarrassing, for she had contributed little to the success of the flight. On their return to the United States, Stultz, Gordon, and Earhart were booked for a thirty-two-city lecture engagement; Amelia grasped the opportunity to promote not only the aviation industry but also independence for women. By the end of the tour the press had dubbed her "Lady Lindy," not only for her courage but because she bore a physical resemblance to aviator Charles Lindburgh.

The next year marked the inaugural of the Women's Air Derby, a kickoff event for the National Air Races. Entry requirements were a pilot's license and at least one hundred hours of flight time. Only thirty women in the entire country were eligible under those conditions, one of whom was Amelia Earhart. The race would cover twenty-eight hundred miles and with no night flying, it would encompass nine full days. Despite mechanical failures, planes catching fire, running out of fuel, and one fatality, fifteen women completed the course with Earhart placing third.

Although negative press haunted the event and assigned the group pejorative labels like "Petticoat Pilots" and "Flying Flappers," the women had established a common bond. Four of the participants formed an association of women fliers, known as the Ninety-Nines, to honor the number of charter members. The group acted as a voice for the inclusion of women in aviation and eventually became an international organization that included most of the women fliers in the world.

In 1931 Amelia Earhart accepted the seventh marriage proposal from her longtime friend and adviser, publisher George Palmer Putnam, with a one-year "escape clause" and several conditions. Always her champion, he became her promoter in earnest after their marriage, and soon her picture graced billboards and products, ranging from clothing to luggage, and she was always flying off somewhere on another promotional tour.

Still feeling somewhat guilty about the attention she received merely for being a passenger on the trans-Atlantic flight, Amelia knew it was time to repeat the feat—this time in the pilot's chair and solo. She had logged more than one thousand hours in the air and was adept at instrumentation. Accompanied by a thermos of soup, Earhart boarded the small, single-engine Lockheed Vega in May 1932, taxied down the runway, and lifted into a clear, blue sky bound for Paris.

Several hours into the flight, cruising at twelve thousand feet, everything began to go wrong. A sudden electrical storm wreaked havoc on her instruments, leaving some disabled, and a sudden drop in temperature caused ice formations on the wings. Spinning out of control, the Vega dropped three thousand feet and virtually skimmed the ocean waves. Amelia managed to reclaim control and altitude, only to observe flames shooting out of the plane's manifold and gas leaking into the cockpit. Knowing she would never make it to Paris, she steered the aircraft northward toward what she hoped was Ireland. At last she sighted land and located a clearing, setting the plane down without incident except for a few badly frightened cows.

She landed near the city of Londonberry and had completed the flight in a little over fifteen hours, establishing a new world speed record and becoming the first woman to go the distance alone. On her return to the United States, she also became the first of her gender to be presented the gold medal of the National Geographic Society, an award placed into her hands by President Herbert Hoover. Eventually she was also the only civilian woman to receive the United States Distinguished Flying Cross. Ironically, considering the horrors of the trip, she titled her book about the flight, *The Fun of It* (1932).

Over the next year she earned a new long-distance time for women in a nonstop flight from Los Angeles to Newark, New Jersey, and then broke her own record on a second trial. In 1935 Earhart became the first pilot, man or woman, to cross the Pacific from Hawaii to Oakland, California, an eighteen-hour jaunt without sleep, and the first woman to navigate from Mexico City to Newark.

Taking a much needed break from the limelight and constant rush of the press and admirers, Amelia spent the next year as an officer of Luddington Lines, the first commercial group to provide regular passenger service between New York City and Washington, D.C. and then accepted an appointment as visiting aeronautics advisor and women's career counselor at Purdue University in Indiana. The sedate world of academe could not hold Earhart's interest for long, however, and even while she nurtured her students, she was planning for her next adventure.

Her time at Purdue proved worthwhile when the university established the Amelia Earhart Research Foundation and purchased a twin-engine Lockheed Electra to outfit as her flying laboratory. The foundation was interested in the effects of prolonged flight on the human body, particularly metabolic rate and fatigue, but Earhart saw the aircraft as the means to launch her greatest exploration, a circumnavigation of the globe at the Equator, a distance of some twenty-nine thousand miles.

After studying maps and weather conditions, changing flight plans, and securing permissions to use the airspace of other countries, the only major hurdle left was selecting a navigator to accompany her. Frederick J. Noonan, a former Pan American Airways pilot, accepted the slot. Earhart had also chosen Carl Allen of the *New York Herald Tribune* to cover the event, and before departure she told him this would be her last flight, for it was time to pass the reigns to a new generation of adventurers.

On June 1, 1937 Earhart and Noonan climbed into the cockpit, even though all repairs to the plane, especially the radio, had not been double-checked. The plane was equipped with seats for ten passengers but those had been jettisoned to store the extra fuel needed for the long legs of the trip; unfortunately, that fuel also added to the weight, making take-offs and landings more awkward.

According to reports sent back and periodic conversations with her husband, Amelia successfully covered twenty-two thousand miles, flying from Miami to South America and over Africa, India, and Australia to Lae, New Guinea, with prearranged stopovers. Departing the jungles of New Guinea, bound for Howland Island and home, the fliers had only seven thousand miles to go. She was to remain in periodic radio contact with the ship *Itasca*, which was tracking her progress and throughout the beginnings of the flight all was well. During the night, however, transmittals began to drift in later than scheduled, then intermittently and static-filled. Desperately, the ship attempted to maintain contact, and at 7:42 A.M., she reported in, stating they were lost, running short of fuel, and flying low. At 8:45 A.M. a frantic message reached the ship stating that the plane was running north and south. Then there was silence.

Beginning immediately with the *Itasca*, the largest search in history was mounted. Over sixteen days with the aid of the United States Navy, ten ships and sixty-five aircraft combed the area, while the mythmakers circulated rumors of her being captured by the Japanese, assuming a new identity, or going underground as a spy. The searchers discovered nothing, no clue, just a wide expanse of ocean.

Realizing the risks she was taking each time she boarded an aircraft, Amelia Earhart always left what she called "popping off" letters addressed to the significant people in her life, to be opened "just in case." When hope ran out, George Putnam tore away the envelope to discover Earhart's last message to the world: "Women must try to do things as men have tried. When they fail, their failure must be but a challenge to others."

References and Suggested Reading

Brink, Randall. *Lost Star: The Search for Amelia Earhart*. New York: Norton, 1994.
Butler, Susan. *East to the Dawn: The Life of Amelia Earhart*. New York: Da Capo Press, 1999.
Earhart, Amelia. *The Fun of It*. New York: Harcourt Brace, 1932.
Lovell, Mary S. *The Sound of Wings: The Life of Amelia Earhart*. New York: St. Martin's Press, 1991.
McGoldrick, Jane R. "Amelia Earhart: The Mystery Lives On." *National Geographic World* (February 1997): 15–23.

Pellegreno, Ann. *World Flight: The Earhart Trail*. Ames: Iowa State University Press, 1971.

Rich, Doris L. *Amelia Earhart: A Biography*. Washington, DC: Smithsonian Institution Press, 1996.

Strippel, Dick. *Amelia Earhart: The Myth and the Reality*. New York: Exposition Press, 1972.

Ware, Susan. *Still Missing: Amelia Earhart and the Search for Modern Feminism*. New York: W.W. Norton, 1994.

Dian Fossey
(1932–1985)

United States
Primatologist

A lthough near the end of her life she was obsessively driven by an almost maternal concern for the primates under her protection, Dian Fossey had laid the groundwork for antipoaching laws throughout Africa. Her work as the world's leading authority on the mountain gorillas of Rwanda, an almost extinct species, focused national and international attention on the plight of the world's depleted wildlife.

Dian Fossey was born in 1932 in San Francisco, the only child of George and Kitty Fossey. When she was three years old, her parents divorced, largely due to her father's drinking, and her mother remarried. Dian did not get on well with her stepfather, Richard Price, and led a rather lonely and isolated existence. With little financial assistance from her family, she enrolled in the preveterinary program at the University of California at Davis but subsequently transferred to San Jose State College, earning her bachelor's degree in 1954 in occupational therapy. After graduation Dian relocated in Louisville, Kentucky, and accepted a position as director of the Occupational Therapy Department at the Kosair Crippled Children's Hospital, where she exhibited a talent for communicating with the children.

From her childhood to her time in college as a prize-winning equestrian, Fossey had loved animals and dreamed of exploring Africa, that vast repository of species in the wild. She read extensively about the continent and was greatly moved by George Schaller's *The Year of the Gorilla* (1961), describing his year-long study of the apes. Schaller was among the first to note the familial bonding among the primates and to point out their gentler side. In 1963 Schaller's work inspired Fossey to take out a bank loan equivalent to her next three years' salary to finance a seven-week safari in Africa. Her ambition was two-fold; she wanted to meet renowned paleoanthropologist Louis Leakey and then to see the giant apes for herself.

With no introduction she arrived at the Olduvai dig in Tanzania as a tourist. Leakey was accustomed to unannounced visitors, and although they were troublesome, he usually tried to accommodate their interest in his work by showing them around. When Dian appeared, he had recently discovered a giraffe fossil of which he was particularly proud. He offered to take her into the pit but in the process she lost her footing, slid down the hillside, sprained her ankle, and landed on top of the giraffe bone. To secure his favor even more, she became ill and regurgitated on the specimen.

After bandaging the ankle, regaining her composure, and retaining a modicum of self-esteem, Fossey departed for the gorillas with Leakey's encouragement. She limped up the ten-thousand foot incline and, peering through the thick foliage, she spied for the first time the creatures that would become her life's work.

Although she would have preferred to stay in Africa, Fossey returned to Kentucky and published several articles about her experience in the *Louisville Courier-Journal*. A few years later Louis Leakey was traveling in the United States and stopped in Louisville for a speaking engagement. Leakey had posited the theory that women work better with primates due to innate empathy, a belief already partially verified by his first researcher, Jane Goodall. Recalling Fossey's interest in the gorillas, he contacted the young woman and offered to underwrite an extended study of the mountain apes. Fossey eagerly accepted and in 1966 she was off to the Congo.

It was not quite the romantic place she had envisioned. A series of volcanic mountains, the Virunga, divide the countries of Zaire and Rwanda. Because it is a tropical region, jungle foliage laces the hillsides, mud from the nearly seventy inches of annual rainfall squishes underfoot and slides away into the mist-shrouded valleys. Slopes are steep and covered with prickling nettles that grasp clothing and pierce the skin. The difficult terrain was further complicated by the thin air of the ten-thousand-foot altitude, especially for the asthmatic smoker. Her life was made lonelier because her only two companions, the camp employees, spoke a language she could not comprehend.

Her surroundings were made more palatable by her proximity to the giant gorillas, and Fossey set to work tracking the animals' paths through the jungle. She approached silently at first, sheltering herself behind trees and making notes from there. When she felt comfortable enough to be seen, she tried mimicking the ape's behavior patterns, hoping she would be accepted but erred when her first gesture was chest beating. Unaware that the sound produced was a danger alarm, Fossey duplicated the pounding on her thighs and panicked the group, causing them to lope away to seek cover. She eventually opted for knuckle-walking, grooming, and more contented sounds, and within six months she was able to get within thirty feet of the gorilla families.

In her enclave on top of the world, Fossey was relatively isolated from the outside and unaware that civil war was brewing on her perimeter. After the rebel leader Moise Tshombe usurped power, soldiers entered her encampment and ordered her to leave. She refused and was escorted away. Held in custody for two weeks, Fossey was placed in a cage on public display. She managed to escape after bribing her guards, but an order was issued for her to be shot on sight if she returned.

It took only two weeks for her to recover from the ordeal, and she was ready to try again, this time on the Rwandan side of the volcanoes.

Because the Rwanda gorillas were relatively unexposed to humans, it took a longer time to gain their confidence, but by crawling toward them on hands and knees, she appeared unthreatening and over time was allowed to sit among them. Eventually the gorillas came to touch her, play with her hair or simply stare into her eyes. Some scientific purists criticized the familiarity she gained with her subjects as having the potential to alter their behavior but Fossey did not care. It was almost as if she had found the family she had never had.

In 1967 Dian Fossey and others established the Karisoke Research Centre for Mountain Gorilla Research. At the time there were less than two hundred fifty of the animals on earth and she studied fifty-one of them. Students from all over the world came to work at the Centre, which lightened her workload. Since there was less for her to do and since she was aware that she needed funds to operate, Dian left her mountain top to pursue a doctorate, knowing that grant monies would be more accessible to her if she had the academic credentials. She was awarded a degree in zoology from Cambridge in 1974.

When she returned to Africa, more of the gorillas had disappeared, picked off by poachers. Gorilla heads were lopped off and sold as trophies, fetching around $1,200 each; hands were severed to become $600 ashtrays for tourists; and zoos were paying top dollar for babies, whom the adult gorillas would fight to the death, if necessary, to protect. In 1978 Fossey found the amputated body of Digit, her favorite gorilla, killed by the poachers. Although she called it "active conservation," Dian gave up collecting data and declared war.

She established the Digit Fund, a conservation group based in Englewood, Colorado, to raise money for the fight to protect the gorillas. The group focused international media attention on the Rwandan apes. For Fosse, however, that was not enough and she began to retaliate. She shot at people who came near the camp; she killed the villager's cattle when they wandered onto the Centre grounds; she kidnaped the child of a suspected poacher; she required her student researchers to be armed; she dismantled the poacher's traps, burned their huts, placed bounties on their heads, and had them brought to her for interrogation. She even spread the tale that she knew black magic and could put curses on people, and others circulated the rumor that she tortured her enemies. The woman who lived on top of a volcano for eighteen years had developed a volcanic temper. Persons began to question her sanity, and in 1979 she was asked to leave the country.

Fossey spent the next few years as an associate professor at Cornell University in Ithaca, New York. While there she completed a manuscript of *Gorillas in the Mist*, published in 1983 and made into a film in 1988. Writing about her adopted family offered some peace, but she longed to return to Karisoke.

Assuming that enough time had passed for the situation to calm down, Fossey went back to Rwanda in 1983 to resume her research, even though she had developed emphysema and required a respirator to breathe. Unfortunately, there were those who had not forgotten. Fossey was found murdered in her cabin on December 26, 1985, her face slashed in two by a machete-like weapon called a *panga*. Friends and associates were convinced the act was committed by one of the poachers, but the Rwandan government, perhaps to protect their own, issued a warrant for the arrest of Wayne McGuire, a doctoral candidate from the University of Oklahoma and Fossey's research assistant. Officials asserted McGuire had murdered his mentor to steal her notes. He managed to exit the country and return to the United States, with which there is no extradition treaty. Over time, opinion on who committed the murder switched more to the poachers, but her assassin was never brought to justice. Fossey was buried in the graveyard she had created at the Centre for the bodies of her beloved gorillas.

Dian Fossey as martyr was more effective than Dian Fossey as ecologist. Shortly after her death the Rwandan government made poaching illegal with a five-year jail sentence as punishment. The gorilla habitat is strictly protected and brings tourism to the region, while the Digit Fund continues to solicit contributions to continue research on mountain gorillas.

References and Suggested Reading

Fossey, Dian. *Gorillas in the Mist*. Boston: Houghton Mifflin. Reprint 2000.

Montgomery, Sy. *Walking with the Great Apes*. Boston: Houghton Mifflin, 1992.

Morrell, Virginia, Patricia Kahn, Toomas Koppel, and Dennis Normile. "Called 'Trimates,' Three Bold Women Shaped Their Field." *Science*, 16 April 1993, 260: 420–426.

Mowat, Farley. *Virunga Passion of Dian Fossey*. Toronto: Bantam Books of Canada, 1988.

———. *Woman in the Mists: The Story of Dian Fossey and the Mountain Gorillas of Africa*. New York: Warner Books, 1987. Reprint 1994.

Clare Mary Francis
(1946–   )

England
Sailor

Although a sickly child and lethargic as a teenager, Clare Francis developed into one of the most recognized sailors on earth, competing in both singlehand and crew contests across the Atlantic and around the world. At the height of media and sponsor attention, she navigated a mid-life change of professions, trading her sails for a pen and becoming a best-selling novelist.

Clare Mary Francis was born in Surrey, England, in 1946. Her father, Owen Francis, was a civil service employee who became the chairman of the London Electric Board. Illnesses of one type or another plagued both sides of the family, and Clare's mother, Joan, worried for her children's health. Giving credence to her mother's fears, Clare was diagnosed with a glandular problem that weakened her and prohibited her from competing in sports of any kind. She did, however, gain enough stamina to dance, and determined to "toughen up," Francis joined the Royal Ballet School. Even though the training regimen served to strengthen her physically, she knew she could not compete with the others in the program, who had been practicing since childhood. Knowing that she did not have a future with a dance company, she dropped out after one year. Francis decided to exchange physical endeavors for mental pursuits and enrolled at University College in London, where she earned a degree in economics. After graduation she accepted a position in market research.

Besides dance, the only other physical activity the young woman had engaged in while she was growing up was sailing. Her family vacationed on the Isle of Wight, where her father taught Clare the rudiments of navigation. At seventeen she owned her first dinghy. Shortly after entering the work force in her early twenties, Clare inherited funds from a great uncle that she invested in a 32-foot sloop, the *Gulliver G.* She often dreamed of sailing long distances and voiced her thoughts to a friend who bet she would not do it. That small wager served as inspiration; Clare quit her job and boarded her boat. Thirty-seven days later she docked in Newport, Rhode Island, having steered a course from Plymouth, England, alone, with no radio, and with no formal training. She did, however, have a surplus of seasickness. To recuperate, she spent the winter in the West Indies, supporting herself by taking tourists on chartered tours.

Having returned to England with salt water flowing freely in her veins, Francis looked for sponsors that would enable her to enter sailing competitions. Her first outing was the 1974 Round Britain Race. She finished in only third place but won the prize when she met French explorer and sailor, Jacques Redon, who became her life partner. In 1975 she placed tenth in *Yachting Monthly*'s excursion to the Azores and back and deemed herself ready for more demanding adventures.

By 1976 The *Observer* Royal Western Singlehanded Transatlantic Race was on the horizon. Having navigated the Atlantic alone once before, Francis felt up for the challenge but she needed a larger boat, which a willing sponsor provided. On a trial run with the new craft, the *Golly*, everything went wrong, including leaks, a broken tiller, an inoperative radio, and problems with the steering mechanism, but Clare optimistically felt the repairs could be made before race time. She was one of only four women in a field of one hundred twenty who entered the twenty-nine day, 2,800-mile contest. The British Broadcasting Company (BBC) was underwriting part of her trip in exchange for an on-site documentary, "The World About Us," and the *Daily Express* was to receive periodic radio transmittals.

After loading supplies and making a last minute safety inspection, Clare was underway. Her first voyage across the Atlantic several years earlier had been relatively uneventful, leisurely in fact, but this trip was not to be so. Only a few miles out she hit a series of gales that quickly demolished the repairs that had been made to the ship. The spinnaker toppled into the water and the boat ran over it. Clare pulled the soaked sail out of the surf and remounted it wet. In forty-foot waves water ran across the deck and into the galley and the boat heeled first to one side and then to the other. When the third gale smashed into the craft, it snapped the steering struts, and Francis had to lash herself to the side of the boat while she leaned over the swirling water to fix the break.

At last the waters calmed but then the fog rolled in. Thinking positively, Clare set a course and fell into a dreamless sleep produced by her forty-eight hour wide-awake battle with nature. When she awoke, the fog had lifted and the sun was sparkling, reflected off the two icebergs the boat had miraculously floated through while she slept.

During the next bout of high winds, the struts were mangled but she managed to bend them back into shape. She knew she should make port for repairs but, even though she was quite certain she was already far behind, she did not want to waste the hours it would take to replace the parts. Limping but still afloat, the *Golly* completed the race in thirteenth place. Francis was the first woman and the first British entry to arrive; in addition, she had toppled the women's time record for the crossing. Her celebratory mood was dampened, however, when she learned that one-third of the entries had dropped out and that two of her peers had died.

Clare Francis decided it was time to retire from sailing and settle down. Jacques took a teaching post; Clare accepted a job with IBM as a lecturer and did some writing. Her memoirs of the Atlantic race were recorded in *Come Hell or High Water*, published in 1977. Retirement was not meant to be, however, because Jacques decided to enter the Whitbread Round the World and he needed a crew. The Round the World encompassed twenty-seven thousand miles and required a seven-month commitment, including three extended stopovers in Africa, New Zealand, and South America. The couple purchased a fifty-foot boat, the size necessary for a crew on a voyage of that length, and fitted it with provisions and personnel. In the midst of preparations the couple decided it was time to get married.

Through doldrums, squalls, and encounters with whales and icebergs, Jacques, Clare, and crew finished the race in fifth place. On their return Clare found out she was pregnant, and they decided to shelve their competitive spirits and truly retire from life on the high seas. After her son was born Clare accepted an assignment to narrate a BBC television series, "The Commanding Sea." Filming required her to travel to intriguing locations. She sailed on a replica of the *Golden Hind*, the ship of Sir Francis Drake, and went aboard the United States aircraft carrier, *Saratoga*. The series was published in book form in 1981.

Drawing on her experience and previous publishing success, Clare Francis resolved to write a novel. By then her marriage was breaking up, and she wanted to spend as much time as possible with her young son. Her first novel, *Night Sky*, was published in 1983 and received well enough that she could devote her time exclusively to creative endeavors. From that point on she has published a book approximately every two years.

In 1987 Clare Francis was diagnosed with myalgic encephalomyelitis (ME), a disease of the immune system. Continuing to write, she added activist to her resume as president of the ME Action campaign. Her novels have been published in twenty-one countries and translated into nineteen languages.

References and Suggested Reading

Francis, Clare. *Come Hell or High Water*. London: Pelham Books, Ltd., 1977.
———. *Come Wind or Weather*. London: Pelham Books, Ltd., 1978.
Uglow, Jennifer. *The International Dictionary of Women's Biography*. New York: Continuum Press, 1982.

Birute Marija Filomena Galdikis
(1948–   )

Canada
Primatologist

T he last selected and the most academically oriented of anthropologist Louis Leakey's "Trimates," Birute Galdikis went to Africa in 1971 to study orangutans, the most isolated and reclusive primate. In addition to observing their behavior, she launched a program to reacclimatize captured orangutans to the wild and fought for laws to ensure their protection.

Birute Marija Filomena Galdikis was born in Wiesbadan, Germany. Her parents, Anatanas and Filomena Galdikis, were of Lithuanian background and emigrated to Canada as refugees of World War II. Anatanas worked in the gold and copper mines of the rugged Canadian west to save enough money to move the family to Toronto when Birute was two years old. She and her three siblings became Canadian citizens.

As a child Birute was a combination of nature lover and bookworm. She combed the city parks and examined the streams for tadpoles and frogs. When she was not out exploring in nature, she read about the outdoors and stories of adventure and animals. Her favorite book, ironically, was *Curious George*. By the time she was in second grade, she had selected her life's path; she wanted to be an explorer—or a ballerina.

When she was seventeen, her family relocated to British Columbia to be closer to California, where they ultimately wanted to settle. Her parents, however, were still Lithuanian and United States immigration quotas for Lithuanians had been met. While they waited, Birute attended the University of British Columbia. When they were allowed to enter the country, the family moved to Los Angeles. Birute worked days, saved money, and attended night classes at Los Angeles City College. When she had accumulated enough funds for tuition, she transferred to the University of California at Los Angeles (UCLA). After earning a summa cum laude bachelor's degree in psychology in 1966, she enrolled in graduate school in anthropology, and worked at the University of Arizona field school on archeological digs in the summers.

One morning she listened as one of her professors talked about a woman (Jane Goodall) who lived among and studied primates. At almost the exact instant, she glanced at the open textbook on her desk, and before her was a red, furry creature and a vision. She would go to the jungle and study orangutans. It did not take long for her plan to become a reality, for only a few months later Louis Leakey lectured at UCLA in 1969.

Galdikis approached Leakey after his lecture, professing her desire to study orangutans. Leakey had long been a champion of women as primatologists, lauding the female's ability to observe the minutest details.

After assessing Birute's sincerity and administering a battery of tests of his own design, the anthropologist offered to raise the funds necessary to send her to Borneo. She rushed home to pack, unaware that it would take more than thirty months for those funds to become available.

During the waiting period, Galdikis devoured every book she could find on orangutans, primatology, and archeology and did preliminary work for her doctorate, which she would receive in 1978. She joined a dig in Yugoslavia and returned via London, where she met both Jane Goodall and Dian Fossey. And she married fellow classmate, Rod Brindamour, who agreed to accompany her to Borneo and serve as photographer for the project.

All the pieces were in place, and in 1971 Birute Galdikis, her new husband, and tons of equipment jetted into the night toward the Borneo Tanjung Puting National Park. Borneo is the third largest island in the world, after Greenland and New Guinea, and the entire island offered little dry land. Most of the island was covered in water or swamp or sludge; thus, any travel was undertaken by boat through what Galdikis called "organic acid soup" or by trudging through murky swamp water up to the chest. When they arrived at the camp, the only lodging provided was a hut covered in tree bark, a structure of dubious origin that became both home, laboratory, and office. They christened the area Camp Leakey, a double meaning, to honor her benefactor and to describe the perpetual dampness of the region.

Alone among primates, which normally band together, orangutans are solitary creatures, with a life span of fifty to sixty years, and primarily arboreal. They live in nests fashioned from tree fronds in the tops of trees and venture out only to hunt for food, often merely swinging from tree to tree. It took more than a week for Birute to locate her first subject. She immediately realized that if she planned to track the primates, she would have to plunge into the dankness of the swamps. When they discerned her presence, the orangutans were unimpressed and greeted her by throwing dead tree branches and fruit at her and by defecating on her head.

Even though she encountered poisonous trees, viruses, and insects; was forced to step carefully in the hut she frequently "shared" with a variety of snakes; and often had to unhitch leeches from her extremities or shake them out of her socks; Galdikis was persistent. It took twelve years for the first orangutan to become accustomed to her presence.

Funded by the National Geographic Society, World Wildlife Federation, the Leakey Foundation, and the New York and Chicago Zoological societies, as well as Earthwatch, a Massachusetts-based scientific organization, Galdikis founded the Orangutan Research and Conservation Project, which rehabilitates captured or wounded primates to the wild. Black marketeering in orangutans is big business with the animals fetching about fifty thousand dollars apiece. Birute has successfully saved and reintroduced more than one hundred creatures to the jungle. In addition, the primatologist persuaded the Indonesian government to declare Tanjung Puting a national park and bring an end to the primate trade in the province. During the period she adopted one orphan, Sugito. Vowing to be the "best orangutan mother" she could be, Birute allowed the small creature to cling to her constantly, which made bathing and changing clothes extremely awkward.

In all, Birute Galdikis has been at the helm of the longest continuous study of primates ever conducted, splitting time between the preserve and teaching posts at Simon Fraser University in Vancouver, British Columbia, and Universitas Nasional in Jakarta. She is the recipient of the Sierra Club's Chico Mendes Award, the Chevron Conservation Award, and the United Nations Global 500 Environmental Achievement Award.

The name orangutan derives from the Malay words "orang" and "hutan," meaning "person of the forest." It is this connection to humans that drives Galdikis—although chimpanzees are a closer DNA match to humans than orangutans, the latter have nearly human eyes. Birute believes that if she can understand their behavior, she can aid humans in interpreting their own.

References and Suggested Reading

Galdikis, Birute M. F. *Reflections of Eden: My Years with Orangutans of Borneo.* Boston: Little, Brown and Company, 1995.

Galdikis, Birute, Nancy Briggs, and Karl Ammann. *Orangutan Odyssey.* New York: Harry N. Abrams, 1999.

Montgomery, Sy. *Walking with the Great Apes: Jane Goodall, Dian Fossey, Birute Galdikis.* Boston: Houghton Mifflin, 1992.

Morell, Virginia, Patricia Kahn, Toomas Koppel, and Dennis Normile. "Called 'Trimates,' Three Bold Women Shaped Their Field." *Science*, 16 April 1993, 260: 420–426.

Jane Goodall
(1934–   )

England
Primatologist

Courtesy of the Library of Congress

T he world's foremost expert on chimpanzees in the wild, ethnologist Jane Goodall conducted the longest study of any animal species in its natural surroundings. After working in Africa for over forty years, Goodall turned to promoting worldwide habitat conservation through lecture tours, television specials for Home Box Office (HBO) and *National Geographic*, and writing.

Jane Goodall was born in London, in 1934, the daughter of Mortimer, an engineer, and Vanne, a homemaker. When she was two years old, a chimpanzee was born in captivity at the London Zoo, and her parents purchased a commemorative stuffed replica for the child. "Jubilee," as it was named, became her favorite toy and is still in her possession. From the very beginning Jane loved animals. At only four years of age she sat inside a hen house for five hours to find out where the eggs came from, exhibiting even then the patience that would become her forte. She was an early reader and at seven she discovered *The Story of Doctor Doolittle* by Hugh Lofting which, coupled with her previous favorites, the Tarzan books, planted a longing for Africa in the child. When her parents divorced, the young girl and her mother went to live with Jane's maternal grandmother in Barnemouth near the English Channel. She played outdoors, rode horses, and formed the Alligator Club with her friends to study nature.

Opting not to go to college, Goodall enrolled instead in secretarial school, primarily because her mother told her a good secretary could go anywhere. She worked in several departments at Oxford University and for a film studio that made documentary films. One day an old school chum, who was living in Kenya, invited Jane to come visit. After adding waitressing to her workload to accumulate money quickly, Goodall sailed from London on the passenger liner *The Kenya Castle*.

In 1957, on the advice of a friend, Jane Goodall applied for a secretarial job with world renown anthropologist Louis Leakey, then the curator of Nairobi's Coryndon Natural History Museum (later the National Museums of Kenya). She was hired and spent some time with Leakey and his wife Mary on digs in the Serengeti Plains. Leakey detected a sincerity in the young woman's love of animals as well as empathy and patience and he made her an offer. He would like to send her to Tanzania for several years to study the behavior of wild chimpanzees. Since ethnology was a relatively new field, her lack of training was less important than her desire and he would raise the funds to make the study possible. Goodall did not hesitate and by 1960, she and her mother, along for company, sighted the Gombe Stream Chimpanzee Reserve, thirty square miles of protected environment, from the deck of a boat touching the shores of Lake Tanganyika.

The early period at Gombe was not easy. Both Jane and Vanne Goodall contracted malaria, and her initial observations of the chimps included the detection of a polio epidemic and a war among the chimpanzee tribes. After four months Vanne returned to England but Jane stayed on. She already had made discoveries that would shake the scientific community. During close scrutiny of the chimpanzees, she watched them tear apart and devour a wild pig and hunt for monkeys, proving conclusively that chimps were not vegetarians as previously thought. In addition, she watched as the chimpanzees fashioned crude tools from sticks to root termites from their nests, a find that destroyed the man-as-toolmaker theory so long held inviolable by animal researchers. This discovery necessitated a reevaluation of evolutionary beliefs.

After almost a year of living among the chimps, Goodall was approached by several of the creatures who had come to understand that she posed no threat. A mother chimp even permitted her baby to touch the researcher. From then on they became her "Banana Club"; she fed them and participated in their activities, such as spending time in trees and munching on insects. Unlike primatologists who would follow her path, Goodall did not infiltrate or manipulate the chimpanzee's daily life and tried to remain a neutral observer. She did, however, come to understand an important key to their social structure: each had a unique personality, and she gave them names on that basis.

In 1961 *National Geographic*, long a supporter of Goodall's research, sent a nature photographer to document her work. The Dutch Baron Hugo van Lawick was so impressed that he mailed his story, took up residence on the reserve, and married Goodall. They had one child, named Hugo after his father but called Grub. As he grew, Grub became jealous of the chimps and had to spend his play time in a wire cage for his own protection. Jane said she modeled her own mothering skills on the behavior of the chimpanzees, for they were loving parents.

While she was taking a short leave to care for her son, Goodall entered Cambridge University in 1965, earning a doctorate and becoming only the eighth person in the history of that institution to do so without a bachelor's degree. Goodall and her son returned to Africa but eventually Grub went to boarding school back in England. Hugo and Jane were divorced in 1974. A few years later Goodall wed Derek Bryceson, a Tanzanian cabinet member, who was director of the national parks.

In 1975, after an attack on the reserve by Zairian rebels, who kidnapped four white student volunteers and held them for ransom, Bryceson and Goodall founded the Jane Goodall Institute, based in Tucson, Arizona, to raise funds to protect the habitat from outside influences. Bryceson died of cancer in 1980, and Goodall decided to dedicate herself to promoting awareness of the importance of worldwide habitat conservation.

By the turn of the century Goodall was spending less time on the reserve and more time traveling to make presentations and visit animals in captivity. An area of particular concern has been the treatment of primates, particularly chimpanzees, in zoos, as pets, as amusements for tourists, and in medical laboratories. Many of those creatures have been left homeless and cannot not be reintroduced into a family unit; thus, Goodall has actively raised funds to create sanctuaries across Africa to house the chimps.

Due in part to her exhaustive studies on the social structure of the groups, she has been particularly discouraged in finding chimps isolated in cages, without room to roam, groom, and socialize with other primates. Because chimpanzees have the closest genetic link to humans, with remarkably similar DNA, they are widely used for medical research. One such facility, the New York University Medical Center Laboratory for Experimental Medicine and Surgery in Primates, houses over two hundred fifty chimps, injecting them with viruses like AIDS and hepatitis and then offering potential treatments. Slowly, the technicians are responding to Goodall's suggestions to furnish larger cages, expose the test animals to the outdoors and contact with each other, and furnish them with toys and video games to alleviate boredom. Her ideal, of course, is to end live animal testing, replacing it with computer models, but until that day she continues to lobby for more humane treatment.

References and Suggested Reading

Arias, Ron. "Jane Goodall." *People Weekly*, 14 May 1990, 33: 93–97.

Goodall, Jane. *Africa in My Blood: An Autobiography in Letters.* Edited by Dale Peterson. Boston: Houghton Mifflin, 2000.

———. *The Chimpanzees of Gombe.* Boston: Houghton Mifflin, 1986.

———. *The Shadow of Man.* Boston: Houghton Mifflin, 1971. Reprint and Revised Edition, 2000.

The Jane Goodall Institute. *www.janegoodall.org*

Lindsey, Jennifer. *Jane Goodall: Forty Years at Gombe.* New York: Stewart, Tabori and Chang, 1999.

Montgomery, Sy. *Walking with the Great Apes.* Boston: Houghton Mifflin, 1992

Morrell, Virginia. "Lost Chimps." *International Wildlife* (September/October 1996) 26: 12–22.

Morrell, Virginia, Patricia Kahn, Toomas Koppel and Dennis Normile. "Called 'Trimates,' Three Bold Women Shaped Their Field." *Science*, 16 April 1993, 260: 420–426.

Ernestine "Dee Dee" Green
(1939–   )

United States
Archaeologist/Environmentalist

As a woman in archeology, Dee Dee Green has come a long way from the shy, insecure child who dreamed of Native American civilizations as she galloped her way around Texas. From surviving a shaman's curse to acquiring a position with the National Forest Service, she has proved her courage and earned her place in what was once a man's world.

Ernestine "Dee Dee" Green was born in Cameron, Texas, in 1939, the daughter of J. Nelson Green, an insurance claims adjuster with a degree in law, and Laverne Green, a secretary. A shy young woman, Dee Dee asked her father to teach her to play baseball to boost her self-confidence. She also learned to ride horses, and during one summer vacation the family visited the Indian pueblos in New Mexico on horseback. She was immediately fascinated and read everything she could find on both the Native Americans of the Southwest and the profession of archaeology.

When Dee Dee was a teenager, a family friend told her about the Panhandle-Plains Historical Museum in nearby Canyon, Texas, and she and several of her friends went in search of history. The museum curator, Dr. Jack Hughes, was impressed with the young woman's enthusiasm and invited her to become a volunteer, which she did every weekend from then on, lassoing a friend or two to help out each time. As a bonus Hughes took the girls on archaeological digs from time to time.

Green attended Texas Technical University in Lubbock, majoring in archaeology. Because she had spent the time with Hughes, she was already ahead of most of her classmates, and her professor asked her to lead an excavation crew of four men at the end of her sophomore year. After transferring to the University of Arizona in 1951, Dee Dee worked in the summer field school at Point of Pines and earned her bachelor's degree in 1961. She acquired an auxiliary interest in scientific illustration, and after taking some preliminary art courses, she received her master's degree in 1963.

Intending to do postgraduate work, Green traveled to the University of Hawaii, but one of the professors there asked her to go to Thailand for six months. Jumping at the chance for fieldwork as well as a trip abroad, Dee Dee accepted the offer and became the leader, once again, of a four-man expedition—only these men did not speak English. Communicating as best they could, the group traversed the previously unexplored regions of the Korat Plateau and examined the tributaries of the Mekong River, a site dating back to prehistory. During their travels, they spent the nights in Buddhist wats, platforms erected on three-foot-high poles with no walls. As the only woman on the trek, Dee Dee soon mastered the fine art of dressing and undressing under a sarong.

As the sole Caucasian on the expedition, she encountered some prejudice among the indigenous population, and one of their shamans put a curse on her for disturbing the natural world. Actually, the curse was not on her directly but on the Land Rover she was driving. When the car's engine turned over on the first try, Dee Dee emitted an audible sigh of relief. Assigned to the region during the Vietnam War, Green also learned to ride a motorcycle in case the party needed to evacuate quickly.

When she returned to the University of Pennsylvania, she had to think before responding in English. She had spent so much time speaking in sign language and broken phrases that she had almost forgotten how to carry on a conversation. As part of her doctoral research, Green explored the Mayan ruins near Tikal, Guatemala. Once again, this was the first Mayan expedition supervised by a woman and she was the only woman to ever backpack into the otherwise inaccessible environs. Despite encounters with tarantulas and jaguars, a sting from a centipede, and battles with trees with poisonous thorns, Dee Dee survived and received her doctorate in 1970.

She accepted a teaching post at Western Michigan University in Kalamazoo and ran their field school in New Mexico during the summer. The field school bordered on United States Forest Service lands, and Dee Dee Green struck up a friendship with the regional archaeologist, ironically named Dee Green.

For relaxation Dee Dee raced sailboats and joined a sailing club, which assigned members without boats to various boats in the races. On one outing club member Rudolph Robles served as her crew. They were married in 1978, whereupon he purchased his own boat and began to compete against his wife. After one year of marriage, Dee Dee received a call from her old friend, Dee Green, informing her of a job opening with the National Forest Service. Even though it meant being separated from her new husband for six months or more until he could change positions, she accepted the offer. Assigned to Missoula, Montana, Dee Dee Green became one of very few women serving as regional archaeologists for the United States government. Even though she was two thousand miles and several months away from her husband, Dee Dee was home.

References and Suggested Reading

Behar, Ruth, and Deborah Gordon, eds. *Women Writing Culture*. Berkeley: University of California Press, 1995.
Golde, Peggy. *Women in the Field*. Berkeley: University of California Press, 1986.
Shapiro, Harry. *Man, Culture and Society*. London: Oxford University Press, 1971.

Beatrice Ethel Grimshaw
(1871–1953)

Ireland

South Pacific Explorer/Journalist

B ored with a career as a successful journalist in Ireland, Beatrice Grimshaw spent thirty years exploring the islands of the South Pacific and the East Indies. She financed her travels through her writing, first as a journalist and then as the author of more than forty books.

Beatrice Ethel Grimshaw was born in 1871 in the city of Cloona, County Antrim, in Ireland. Little is known of her childhood or her parents; however, it can be assumed from her educational background that she came from wealth. Grimshaw was educated at Victoria College in Belfast, at Pension Retailaud in Caen, France, at the University of Belfast, and at Bedford College in London. As a young woman she set a new twenty-four-hour world record as a cyclist and became a respected journalist.

Always wanting to travel and explore, Beatrice accepted a position with the London *Daily Graphic* to travel around the world and report on her experiences. In addition, she secured free passage from shipping companies in return for press coverage of her trip. Her world tour was truncated, however, for the moment she landed in the South Pacific, she lost any desire to journey farther.

After touring Tahiti she selected Papua, New Guinea, as her home base in 1907. Living in a series of houses she built herself, Grimshaw explored the untamed, unexplored inland regions of that island. She became the first white woman to go up the Sepik River, one of the world's largest waterways and the home of several specialized religious groups, the Maio Yam Cult, and the Swagup or insect people. In 1909 she went diving in the Torres Straights, an unparalleled experience for a woman of her generation.

She ran a coffee plantation, became the first woman to grow tobacco on the island, and tried her hand at diamond prospecting, always carrying a revolver tied around her waist. Earning her independence through her writing, Grimshaw published over forty books, some travel oriented and some purely romances and adventures. She was a serious student of local legends and customs and weaved those into the texts of her work. Her best-known travel book is *From the Fiji to the Cannibal Islands* (1907) and her most popular novels are *The Red Gods Call* (1910) and *The Victorian Family Robinson* (1934).

Once she was asked to join a group of missionaries who were searching for a missing one of their number whom they feared had been captured by cannibals. The fear was evidently justified, for all they found were parts of the man. Over the next three decades, she toured Fiji, the

Solomon Islands, and the islands of Southeast Asia but always returned to New Guinea.

Over time, Grimshaw became a recognized authority on tropical colonization. In 1939 she retired to Australia and lived there until her death.

References and Suggested Reading

Robinson, Jane. *Wayward Women: A Guide to Women Travellers*. New York: Oxford University Press, 1990.

Uglow, Jennifer S. *The International Dictionary of Women's Biography*. New York: Continuum Press, 1982.

Marguerite Elton Baker Harrison (1879–1967)

United States

Spy

One of the founders of the Society of Woman Geographers, Marguerite Harrison went from the sheltered life of an affluent young woman to the intrigue of being held in a Soviet prison as a spy. Created of sheer pluck and luck, Harrison's life story reads like a political thriller in which she, as protagonist, is a visionary, predicting events to come through her observations of existing conditions.

Marguerite Elton Baker Harrison was born in Baltimore, Maryland in 1879. Her father, Bernard Nadal Baker, was a shipping magnate, and the young woman was raised in an atmosphere of wealth with servants and summers in Europe. Her mother was only nineteen when Marguerite was born; thus, there was little mother-daughter interaction between the two, with the exception of a hypochondriacal obsession about the child's health. Marguerite was not allowed playmates for fear of contracting something from one of them. On the other hand, she did have a strong bond with her father, whom she adored.

To prepare for her debut into society and the arrangement of a proper marriage, Harrison was sent to Radcliffe for one year. It was the first experience of independence in her young life, and she celebrated by becoming engaged to her landlady's son. That relationship was short lived, however, for the moment her parents got whiff of her impropriety, they yanked her out of school and whisked her off to Italy for an extended visit. On her return she had her debut and married Thomas Bullitt Harrison, an acceptable husband in her parents' eyes.

In 1915 Marguerite Harrison's world came tumbling down. Her mother died and her father lost the family fortune through a series of bad investments. Then her husband died, leaving her penniless and deeply in debt and with a thirteen-year-old son to support. Initially she converted her home into a boarding house, but that income was insufficient. One day, with only a letter of introduction from her brother-in-law Albert Ritchie, who would become the governor of Maryland, Harrison marched into the *Baltimore Sun* and applied for a job as a journalist. Much to her surprise, she was hired as assistant society editor, despite the fact that she had no training except one semester of college, had never written anything, and could not type. She was a quick study, however, and was promoted to music and drama critic and then appointed to the state board of motion picture censors. During World War I Harrison was assigned to cover the roles of women in the war effort. To add credibility to her research, she went undercover as a streetcar operator and a skilled laborer for Bethlehem Steel.

Of all the countries she had visited as a young woman, she most wanted to return to Germany, but because of World War I that was an impossibility in 1918. If she could not go as a tourist, however, she could as an employee of the United States, and Harrison volunteered her services to the Army Military Intelligence Division (MID) as a spy. The war ended while her paperwork was being processed, but she was sent anyway to report on political and economic matters that might pertain to Army intelligence.

In her guise as journalist, Harrison was the first English-speaking woman correspondent to reach Berlin following the Armistice. The 1919 Peace Treaty at Versailles ended her tenure in Germany. She found the terms of the treaty too lax for she had foreseen trends in the country, particularly a rise in anti-Semitism, that would later lead to World War II.

Although she was notified of the death of her father, Harrison decided to remain in Europe and accepted a new assignment in Russia. She had to enter the country without a visa, but because she was a woman traveling alone, she was passed from one checkpoint to the next as an "oddity," thus, navigating all the way to Moscow. Still acting as a card-carrying reporter, Marguerite attended a speech by Lenin and interviewed Trotsky. She was unaware that her activities were being closely monitored.

One day guards arrived at her home and she was arrested. In the interrogation room she was told the Soviets had proof that she had been a spy in Germany and was a threat to Russia; however, they would grant her freedom if she agreed to counterspy on the foreign visitors who were staying at her guest house. To buy time, she accepted the offer, fabricated reports, and tried to get a message out to her contacts in the Army.

In 1920 Harrison was arrested again. She spent ten months in Lubianka, the institution written about later by Soviet author Aleksandr Solzhenitsyn in *The Gulag Archipelago*. The first American woman ever held in a Bolshevik prison, prisoner #2961 spent much of the time in solitary confinement until she became ill. She was transferred to Novinsky prison, where conditions were somewhat improved, and was eventually released through the intervention of the American Relief Administration (ARA) in exchange for food for the starving peoples of Russia. Harrison reported to the army that the United States needed to recognize the Communist government because it would be essential for trade; as usual, her prognosis was years ahead of its time.

Only ten months later Marguerite accepted a magazine assignment to investigate conditions in the Far East. She sailed around the world to Japan, completing *Unfinished Tales from a Russian Prison* (1923) en route. In a stopover at Alexandrovsk, she was the only woman at a state dinner with twenty Japanese officers. She toured Sakhalin, which had been a Russian penal colony when it was part of Siberia. Only one other American journalist had ever been to the site, and no reporter had been permitted there for over two years.

From there she entered Siberia, taking a paddle wheeler six hundred miles up the Amur River, where she caught a train to Vladivostok. The trip was grueling, for the train constantly rerouted to avoid bandits and bombed-out trestles. Continuing her travels, she circuited Korea, Manchuria, and China.

Something in Harrison drew her like a magnet back to Russia, even though she knew that an appearance within those borders would place her in imminent danger. The region of Chita in Siberia had been independent since the Bolshevik Revolution, and although it was situated within Soviet borders, Harrison was determined to go, in spite of having to slip in, unnoticed, by a most circuitous path. She drove across Mongolia, traversing the Gobi Desert and maneuvering through spots where the vehicle literally hung over mountain ledges or was mired in sand. In Urga she detoured to tour the monastery, known as the seat of the Living Buddha. The next four hundred miles were by horse and carriage, under the constant threat of attack by two-legged and four-legged predators, bandits and wolves. In Verkhne, Udinsk, she spent the night in a brothel and finally reached Chita.

Harrison was arrested almost immediately and transferred to Moscow. When she refused to defect, she was tried for espionage and high treason. She was found guilty, of course, and held for ten weeks until she was spotted and identified by an American Relief Administration (ARA) officer who negotiated her release. The trip and her rearrest were documented in *Red Bear or Yellow Dragon*, published in 1924.

By 1925 Marguerite Harrison was ready for a new undertaking, and with her friend Merian Cooper became the first woman to tackle the fledgling enterprise of documentary film making. Deciding they wanted to record "humans adapting for survival in marginal conditions," they debated about studying either of two groups of indigenous populations, the pastoral Bakhtiari of Persia and the Kurds of Anatolia (Turkey). After deciding on the latter, they visited the site but, finding nothing of interest to film, soon traveled to Persia. There they joined the Bakhtiari nomads on their annual migration over Zardeh Kuh and the Yellow Mountains, including a trek up fifteen thousand feet of solid ice. The march seemed to take place only because it always had, and Harrison referred to the group as "stoics resigned to their destiny." The documentary, entitled *Grass*, was released to underwhelming critical response but has since become a classic of the genre.

The same year Harrison joined four other women explorers to form the Society of Woman Geographers and aided in the establishment of the Children's Hospital School in Baltimore, which she called her greatest accomplishment. In 1926 at age forty-seven, she married Arthur Middle

Blake, an English actor. They moved to Hollywood in order for him to find work. When he died, she returned to Baltimore.

At age seventy-eight Harrison traveled through South America, and in her eighties she returned to Berlin alone. She died of a stroke in 1967 at the age of eighty-eight.

References and Suggested Reading

Harrison, Marguerite. *There's Always Tomorrow: The Story of a Checkered Life*. New York: Farrar & Rinehart, 1938.

Olds, Elizabeth Fagg. *Women of the Four Winds*. Boston: Houghton Mifflin, 1985.

Society of Woman Geographers Web site. *http://www.iswg.org/*

Mae Carol Jemison
(1956–)

United States
Astronaut/Physician

Courtesy of NASA

By age thirty Mae Jemison had received a medical degree, served two years in the Peace Corps, and been selected by the National Aeronautics and Space Administration (NASA) for training as a missions specialist. In 1992 she became the first African American woman to fly in space.

Mae Carol Jemison was born in 1956 in Decatur, Alabama, but the family moved to Chicago when she was three. Her father, Charlie, a roofer and carpenter, and her mother, Dorothy, an elementary school teacher, encouraged their children to educate themselves and reach for the stars, which Mae took literally. When others of her age were out playing stick ball in the streets, young Mae was curled up with a book, devouring material on anthropology, archaeology, evolution, and astronomy.

She graduated from high school at age sixteen with a National Achievement Scholarship in hand for college. Although accepted at the Massachusetts Institute of Technology (MIT), she decided to enroll at Stanford University in 1973. California in the early 1970s was a whole different world from Chicago, and for the first time Jemison encountered prejudice because of both her race and gender. In order to overcome both obstacles, she worked hard, became involved in extracurricular activities on campus, and made excellent grades. She was awarded a bachelor of science degree in 1977 in chemical engineering and African American studies.

Pursuing an interest she had developed in high school, Jemison applied to and was accepted at Cornell University Medical School in Ithaca, New York, where she specialized in biomedical engineering research. While there, she became preoccupied with international medicine and served as president of the Cornell Chapter of the National Student Medical Association, through which she organized a citywide health and law fair in 1979. In 1980 Mae Jemison journeyed to Thailand and worked in a Cambodian Refugee Camp, then received a grant to travel in Kenya, providing primary medical care.

After earning her medical degree in 1981, Jemison worked in general practice in Los Angeles but resigned to join the Peace Corps, where she served from 1983 to 1985. Assigned to Sierra Leone and Liberia, she was the youngest person, at age twenty-six, ever to be named area medical officer. In addition, she managed health care for Peace Corps and United States embassy personnel and did research, including the development of a Hepatitis B vaccine, in conjunction with the Centers for Disease Control in Atlanta.

Although she had considered the step earlier, perhaps it had always been on her mind, the young doctor decided she was seasoned enough to apply for the NASA space program in 1985. When she was accepted into the program in 1987, Jemison was one of only fifteen selected from close to two thousand applicants, one of only four African American astronauts working for NASA, and the first black woman to enter the training. She was hired as a missions specialist, more as a scientist than an astronaut. Missions specialists conduct experiments in space, launch satellites, and walk outside the space craft.

Following a year of intensive training in Houston, Jemison toiled for five years before her first flight. She was instrumental, during that time, in establishing a cooperative mission between the United States and Japan, the spacelab-J project. In 1992 the space pioneer boarded the shuttle *Endeavor* and rocketed into the stratosphere, orbiting the earth one hundred twenty-seven times and conducting experiments with biofeedback on motion sickness.

After returning to earth the first African American woman in space was treated to a six-day, city-wide tribute in her home town of Chicago. Back in Houston, she founded the Jemison group, which develops and markets medical technology. Although she has received numerous awards and belongs to many professional organizations, her most important work is as a role model for young African Americans. She encourages them with her own life motto—"Don't be limited by others' limited imaginations"—and promotes space travel as a new route for breaking through color barriers. As a self-designated "womanist," Jemison supports equality for women, particularly proselytizing to alter the image of women in science.

References and Suggested Reading

Creasman, Kim. "Black Birds in the Sky: The Legacies of Bessie Coleman and Dr. Mae Jemison." *The Journal of Negro History* (Winter 1997) 82: 158–169.

Haynes, Karima, and Marilyn Marshall. "Mae Jemison: Coming in from Outer Space." *Ebony* (December 1992) 48: 188–121.

Interview (July 1993): 75.

"Mae C. Jemison." *Current Biography* (July 1993) 54: 22–26.

Marshall, Marilyn. "Child of the '60s to Become First Black Woman in Space." *Ebony* (August 1989) 44: 50–54.

Amy Johnson
(1903–1941)

———————————————————▶

England
Aviator

Courtesy of the Library of Congress

There was no fanfare, no marching bands, and no cheering crowds when the young secretary turned aviator, still a novice, and boarded her plane bound from London to Australia in 1930, the first flight on that route attempted by a woman. By the time she was halfway to her destination, however, Amy Johnson had become the darling of the press and one of the best-known fliers in Britain.

Amy Johnson was born in the British port city of Hull, the daughter of a fish merchant. As a child and a young woman, she was competitive in school and in sports, playing a rough game of field hockey and infiltrating the male-dominated enclave of cricket. In 1922 she entered Sheffield University, atypical for a woman of her period and economic standing. Despite earning a bachelor's degree in economics, the only jobs open to her were low-paying secretarial positions, one of which, of necessity, she accepted in a London law firm.

In the spring of 1928 Johnson decided to take flying lessons, even though it would cost every penny she earned. She joined the London Aeroplane Club, and eventually earned her private license, even though she was still having trouble with her landings. Her parents encouraged her to become a commercial pilot but she had other plans. She convinced the rather gruff airport ground engineer to take her on as his maintenance apprentice. Beginning at six every morning, before the start of her secretarial job, Johnson dismantled, cleaned, and reassembled aircraft engines. In 1929 she became the first woman in England to pass the test for the British Ground Engineers' License, a full-fledged mechanic.

The old competitive spirit of her youth returned, and Amy Johnson resolved to put her new skill to use by breaking a world record, a flight from London to Australia. At the time she had only eighty-five hours in the air, and the longest trip she had completed was one hundred forty-seven miles; the trip she proposed to take was over ten thousand miles, soaring over sea, desert, mountains, and jungle. Potential sponsors chuckled patronizingly. When door after door closed, she began a letter-writing campaign to the peerage and other notables. Lord Wakefield, a wealthy oil merchant, finally agreed to put up half the monies needed to purchase a plane if Johnson could secure the other half. With her father's contributing the balance, she bought a converted deHavilland Moth, a single-engine plane with only a one-hundred-horsepower engine and an open cockpit. Amy named her aircraft *Jason* to honor her dad, not his name but the logo of the fish market, the Greek Argonaut.

There was only a smattering of well wishers at the airport to see her off, and the first few hours went smoothly. On the third day, however, she was flying over Turkey and nearing the Taurus Mountains, her first major obstacle. She was forced to carry extra fuel on board, and the added weight would not allow the tiny craft to gain more than ten thousand feet in altitude; the mountains were eleven thousand feet. She had to zoom down the canyon, blindly seeking passes and hoping her wings did not scrape the rock cliffs jutting out from the mountainsides. Navigating well, she relaxed and then the world disappeared. The plane was engulfed in a cloud bank and visibility was zero. After only a few minutes, it soared free of the fluff just as one wing was heading straight toward a rock wall. She managed to bring the craft around and noticing a railroad track far below, followed its route through the pass.

Near Baghdad a sand storm hit the plane. More hazardous than winter blizzards, sand storms can instantly block visibility. Roaring into the open cockpit, the sand permeated all of the controls and blacked out her goggles. Having no other choice, Johnson headed down, landing at full throttle and damaging the underbelly. She climbed out, sat on the tail, weighting down the vehicle so that it would not be blown away, and endured three hours of the storm. She was not aware that, at the very moment back in England, the press was singing her praises and calling her "The Flying Secretary."

Landing having never been her long suit, Amy had other close encounters throughout her journey. She ran low on fuel and broke a wing in the process of touching down. In Rangoon she landed on a soccer field, slid across and stopped nose down in a ditch. During a rainstorm she set the plane down in Java in a sugar plantation and hopscotched over stakes sticking up in the ground. She mended the tears in the bottom of the plane with adhesive tape. Johnson arrived in Australia hours over the record she had hoped to best, but as the first woman ever to complete the flight solo. She returned to England a national hero. She was offered gifts, presented the Royal Order of the British Empire, and asked by the *Daily Mail* to publish pieces on her flight as well as to make personal appearances.

In 1931 Amy Johnson broke the time record from England to India and the speed record for light planes on a flight from London to Tokyo via Moscow, making that circuit in only ten days. Her marriage the next year to famed pilot Jim Mollison brought another barrage of media attention with headlines lauding the couple as "The Flying Sweethearts."

After Johnson broke her husband's record from London to Cape Town, Mollison thought it best for his ego if they flew together. Their first team outing was a record flight across the Atlantic in 1933, with a scheduled return route via Baghdad. The shared flight reached North America, but after running out of fuel the plane set down near Bridgeport, Connecticut, short of the New York City destination, skidded off the runway, and smashed into a swamp. Even though the plane was beyond repair, the time record was broken and "The Flying Sweethearts" were feted with a White House reception, meeting Franklin and Eleanor Roosevelt as well as famed American aviator Amelia Earhart.

Their next attempt at a joint venture was a 1934 entry in the England-Australia trophy race. Although they were in first place during the initial half of the run, mechanical difficulties forced them to withdraw midway. Wherever they traveled Johnson was in the limelight and her fame overshadowed Mollison's. As a result, the couple divorced in 1938.

When her marriage ended Johnson, who had always shied away from attention, retired and purchased a home in the country to do some writing. But with the advent of World War II, she volunteered for the Women's Auxiliary Air Force as part of the Air Transport Auxiliary. In 1941 an aircraft she was ferrying was long overdue when a plane was spotted over the Thames Estuary, spiraling toward the water. The ship HMS *Haslemere* was on convoy duty on the river. The captain immediately altered his course to rush toward the scene but hit a sandbar and had to dislodge before proceeding. When the ship arrived at the site, some of the crew reported hearing a woman's voice plead, "Hurry, please hurry," and momentarily sighted the downed pilot. Then, the figure disappeared. No body was ever found and the plane sank quickly, thus making positive identification impossible. Although it would have meant Amy Johnson was over one hundred miles off course, floating debris from the wreckage bore her name.

References and Suggested Reading

Babington-Smith, Constance. *Amy Johnson*. London: Collins, 1967.
Johnson, Amy. *Sky Roads of the World*. London: W & R Chambers, 1939.

Mary Henrietta Kingsley
(1862–1900)

→

England

Africa Explorer/Humanitarian

T he most Victorian of the Victorian women travelers, Mary Kingsley explored areas of Africa where no European, particularly no
woman, had ever been. She fearlessly traversed the continent,
moving between villages, sailing down rivers, trekking up mountains,
collecting fish and insects, and acquiring a deep understanding of the
indigenous peoples.

Mary Henrietta Kingsley was born in the Islington section of London,
England, in 1862. Her father, George, was a physician who made "house-
calls" to important personages living abroad, which gave him the opportunity to pursue his true passion, that of amateur anthropologist.
However, her uncle and George's brother, Charles Kingsley, author of
Westward Ho! and other works, was the more famous of the clan. Mary's
mother, also named Mary, had been her father's housekeeper until her
pregnancy was discovered. After they were married, he became estranged from his family, who disapproved of the union.

Because her father was seldom at home and her mother was ill and
often bedridden, the young woman forfeited her early years to function
as housekeeper, nurse, and companion to her mother and brother. She
was essentially self-educated, although she did manage to slip away
from her duties to take sociology courses at Cambridge University. In
1893 both of her parents died within months of one another, and at age
thirty-one, Mary Kingsley was free to do as she liked.

Recalling her father's tales of his travels and his love of foreign peoples
and thinking about her own attraction to natural history, Kingsley decided it was time to explore the world. She began with a trip to the
Canary Islands. There, she watched as others boarded ships bound for
West Africa and had an overwhelming desire to be among them. She
wanted to pursue her own interests in religious practices and to complete
a book her father had been writing at his death; unfortunately, she had
no money for such an expedition.

In her readings she had stumbled across *A Study of Fishes* by a Dr.
Gunther, who was affiliated with the British Museum and had apolo-
gized to his readers for the insufficient information on African species
in his book. Kingsley called on the man and offered her services to complete his research. Much to her surprise, he accepted and offered her
museum funding for the trip. Although her brother assumed she would
now become his housekeeper, Mary Kingsley boarded a ship to study
fish and fetishes on the Dark Continent.

Decked out in a high-necked blouse, snug sealskin hat, buttoned
leather boots, and a long black wool skirt, she ventured into the swel-

tering jungles and along the rivers of West Africa, armed only with an umbrella and her gentle nature. She was limited by a lack of maps and not permitted to tour some of the areas she would have liked to visit, but the first journey was sufficient to whet her appetite for more. She returned to London with an impressive amount of information and enough samples of fish to convince the museum to underwrite a second expedition, this time inland to search for insects.

In 1895 Kingsley returned to Africa after befriending her passenger ship's captain and crew and learning rudimentary navigation and cargo storage from them. She was even allowed to pilot the two-thousand-ton vessel for a short run off the African coast. Hiring a group of native bearers, she plunged inland to parts hitherto unvisited by Europeans. She walked through jungles, waded through swamps, canoed on rivers, and encountered a variety of wildlife from crocodiles to leopards and gorillas. Paying visits to amazed chiefs and shamans, she earned their confidence by bartering rum, gin, and fish hooks for ivory and rubber and traded these elsewhere along the route. Often depending on native hospitality for lodging, she slept in unusual places, including one hut containing a bag filled with human remains. She traveled one hundred forty miles up the Ogowe River into the unknown territory of the Great Forest and the home of the Fang, considered the most primitive of the inland peoples and reputed to be cannibals. Perhaps because Kingsley was a white woman or because her garb was so peculiar, she encountered no animosity and escaped death.

On the return trek Kingsley climbed Mt. Cameroon, over thirteen thousand feet high. She was not the first but it was still considered an admirable undertaking for an untrained mountaineer and a woman of her age. Once, while seeking specimens of beetles for the museum, she tumbled into a fifteen-foot-deep animal trap with ebony spikes embedded in the bottom. She was saved from certain death only by the voluminous folds of fabric in her heavy skirt. Throughout her travels she investigated witchcraft, cannibalism, the status of women, death rites, animism, and pantheism, but her primary concern was the condition of the native peoples and her desire to leave them unspoiled.

After going back to England Kingsley gave a series of lectures on her travels and discoveries. Her emphasis in these presentations always underscored her conviction that European culture should not be imposed on Africa and that the governors needed a stronger understanding of local religions, laws, and customs. She firmly stated her disagreement with missionaries who attempted to change moral standards and with traders and politicians who exploited the natives. In addition to her public lectures, she published *Travels in West Africa* (1897), chronicling her thousand-mile journey, and *West African Studies*, a treatise on the need to assume a hands-off policy on change.

Not a feminist, as were many of her contemporaries, Mary Kingsley sat silently by while a male colleague read her paper to a scientific gathering where women were allowed no voice. She publicly condemned the efforts of other women to gain access to these male-dominated societies and eschewed personal glory connected with her explorations. Her only concern was humanitarian: to protect the culture of Africa.

Preparing to undertake a third expedition, Kingsley heard reports of the outbreak of the Boer War in Africa and of the devastation, injuries and casualties produced by the confrontation. She abandoned her thoughts of an excursion and rushed to be of aid. When she arrived at the Palace Barracks in Simon's Town, Cape Town, South Africa, there was one doctor and two nurses on duty to attend to the more than two hundred wounded prisoners of war. The facility was infested with crawling insects and lice, and an epidemic of typhoid swept from one patient to another. Although she was aware that caring for the typhoid victims would put her danger, Mary Kingsley continued her work even after she contracted the disease.

Understanding that she was near death, she instructed the doctor on duty to bury her at sea. Her body was transported three miles offshore on the HMS *Thrush* and with full military honors, the coffin was lowered onto the waves. Someone, however, had neglected to weight the now bobbing box and a lifeboat with the extra ship's anchor was lowered to assure her final rest. She was thirty-eight years old. A few years after her death, the Mary Kingsley Hospital was opened in Liverpool, England, for the treatment of tropical diseases.

References and Suggested Reading

Blunt, Alison. *Travel, Gender and Imperialism: Mary Kingsley and West Africa*. New York: Guilford Press, 1994.

Frank, Katherine. *A Voyager Out: The Life of Mary Kingsley*. Boston: Houghton Mifflin, 1986.

Middleton, Dorothy. *Victorian Lady Travelers*. New York: E. P. Dutton and Company, 1965.

Oliver, Caroline. *Western Women in Colonial Africa*. Westport, CT: Greenwood Press, 1982.

Monica Kristensen
(1950–   )

Norway
Antarctic Explorer

I n an attempt to re-create Roald Amundsen's first trek to the South Pole, Monica Kristensen lead a team of men across the frozen terrain with grit and determination, despite a series of obstacles that would have caused others to abandon the quest. Although they did not reach their goal and encountered a barrage of negative press, the expedition was considered the most scientifically significant polar expedition of the modern era.

Monica Kristensen was born in 1950 in Torsby, Sweden, but raised in Oslo by her Norwegian father, a station master. As a child she took long treks to the mountains, read compulsively, and trained a team of huskies. She attended the University of Oslo, receiving an undergraduate degree in mathematics and quantum physics, then enrolled at the University of Tromso to study theoretical plasma physics.

While working on her degree, she was assigned to the research station of the Norwegian Polar Institute on the edge of the Arctic. She was the only woman among six men, a team of drillers with the King's Bay Mining Company, and polar bears of both genders. Her assignment was to record the patterns of the aurora borealis, and watching from a small wooden hut on stilts, she gave up sleep due to the constant observation required. During down time, she learned mushing, the art of driving sled dogs, and wrote short stories that were gathered in *The Magical Land* (1978).

To become a glaciologist, Kristensen was required to conduct research on icebergs. She made two voyages to Antarctica aboard the HMS *Endurance*, the Royal Navy's ice patrol ship, where she was once again the sole woman surrounded by one hundred twenty-five men. It was during those expeditions that she decided to re-create Roald Amundsen's trek to the South Pole.

In 1983, with a diploma in polar studies and a doctorate in antarctic tabular icebergs, Kristensen began to organize the expedition. She brought together a British advisory board, all past presidents of the Royal Geographical Society, enlisted her best friend Neil McIntyre, and purchased twenty-two Greenland huskies. The dogs would pull two sledges with supplies, while Kristensen and three men skied behind. All was going well and then everything went wrong.

She had asked the National Science Foundation (NSF), a United States agency that oversees scientific research and mans four bases in Antarctica, to fly the party, dogs included, to the starting point and to later pick up the team. The request was denied. According to some sources, transporting the dogs was problematic, while others cited NSF's view that the expedition was of little scientific merit. Following that disappointment, Neil became extremely ill and Monica hurt her knees in a car crash with her fiancé, Arne Solas. The two other members of the team gave up.

Determined to go on, Kristensen located replacements for the explorers, Jacob Larsen and Jan Almquist, and arranged to transport equipment and supplies by ship, but this vessel sank. Realizing she could no longer rely on others, she purchased a one-thousand-ton Newfoundland ice breaker, which she christened *Aurora*. Already a month behind schedule, the group got underway in 1986, but the expedition was still cursed. Shortly after departure, two thousands gallons of diesel fuel dumped into the ship's hold, saturating food, supplies, and explosives with sticky liquid. They had to stop briefly to clean the ship and salvage what they could, but while those tasks were being completed, the ship froze in the ice and was immovable for several days.

Nine days later the group sighted the Ross Ice Shelf, a shimmering wall of frozen water reaching one hundred feet up to the sun, then diving nine hundred feet down into the sea. The supplies had already been flown in and ski landed, and the National Geographic Society had sent a film crew to record their departure for an hour-long documentary.

The distance across the Ice Shelf was 530 miles, roughly the size of a small country, and included the 9,000-foot Axel Heiberg Glacier, which would have to be climbed. Shortly after the expedition began in earnest, there was a dog fight on one of the sledges, leaving one wounded husky that had to be carried. There were crevasses and spots of broken ice along the way that produced constant rerouting, and the four explorers were putting in twelve-hour days followed by the paperwork necessitated by research.

The plane had placed food and supplies at strategic checkpoints en route to cut down on weight on the sledges, but when the group reached the Transarctic Mountains, they could not find the third checkpoint. After looking for four days and listening to hungry dogs howling and their own stomachs growling, they were on the verge of turning back and recalling the tales of Amundsen's eating one of his dog teams to stay alive. Just as time was running out, the supplies were discovered buried in snow. At one point the sun popped out and Kristensen had the once-in-a-lifetime experience of skiing on a rainbow as the light reflected a prism on the snow.

When they reached the Axel Heiberg Glacier, the ascent was steeper than they had expected, and they had to camp four times during the climb. In order to sleep, the party was forced to tie themselves down to keep from sliding downhill. Kristensen developed frostbite and was constantly overheated due to the exertion of mounting the glacier.

The group reached a point where they had to make a decision about continuing and voted to turn back without going on to the Pole. By that time the expedition was over a month behind schedule, and if they did not return to the ship, it would be icebound and they would be wintering in Antarctica, an unpleasant prospect, particularly considering there would be no sun for three months. The return trip was less eventful with the exception of the sledge's overturning and Monica falling, sliding, and literally sailing over a crevasse.

On their return some lauded their exploits as being of heroic proportions, while others labeled them failed amateurs. Although disillusioned by her failure to reach the Pole, Kristensen was pleased that she had endured and proven she had the right stuff. In 1988 she married Arne Solas and began a series of archaeological expeditions in Norway.

References and Suggested Reading

Macklin, Debbie. "Queen of the Poles." *New Scientist*, 24 June 1989, 122: 79–80.
Melchett, Sonia. *Passionate Quests: Five Modern Women Travellers.* Boston: Faber and Faber, 1992.
Satchell, Michael. "Trying to Recap Antarctic Daredevilry." *U.S. News & World Report*, 16 February 1987, 102: 75–76.

Anne LaBastille

United States
Ecologist

Photo by Frank DiMeo. Courtesy of Anne LaBastille

Although she is known as a woodswoman, the title or subtitle of three of her published works on ecology, Anne LaBastille is much more than a Henry David Thoreau clone living in an isolated cabin on the fringes of the frontier. She has invested years in traveling the world as a conservationist, planning national parks and reserves, fighting to save species from extinction, and promoting public awareness of the fragile balance between humans and nature.

Anne LaBastille was born in New York City and raised in suburban New Jersey. According to the introduction of *Woodswoman* (1976), her first glimpses of the wilderness were at Girl Scout camp, Camp Fire Girls retreats, and the local golf course. She dreamed of escaping to nature, and as a teenager she secured a summer job teaching horseback riding in the Adirondack Mountains of upstate New York, an area she would eventually consider home. Returning to that area after college, she married Morgan Brown, and for the duration of their time together, she aided him in managing a lodge there. LaBastille attended Cornell University in Ithaca, New York, receiving a bachelor's degree in conservation of natural resources. From there she journeyed to Colorado State University in Fort Collins for a master's, directing a winter study of mule deer for her thesis project. She returned to New York and earned a doctorate in wildlife ecology from Cornell University.

As a young woman LaBastille led nature tours into the wilderness areas of the Caribbean and Central America. While on one of those treks in Guatemala, she was intrigued by an endemic species, the giant pied-billed grebe, a bird that existed only in the reed beds of Lake Atitlan. The bird, called "poc" by the local population, was in danger of disappearing because large mouth bass had been introduced in 1960 and they were devouring the smaller fish and crabs which comprised the grebes' diet.

Her first count of the water fowl netted only ninety-nine, and she resolved to create a sanctuary, monitor the population, and, if necessary, begin a conservation campaign. The Mayan population labeled her "Mama Poc" but often quietly referred to her as the "crazy bird lady." Undeterred, Anne obtained grants from the World Wildlife Fund and the Smithsonian Institution and set to protecting the reed bed habitat and the grebes. Having successfully accomplished those goals, she persuaded the Guatemalan government to designate the grebes' habitat as the country's first wildlife sanctuary.

Steadily, the numbers improved until natural and manmade disasters struck. During the 1970s the lake became a resort area and condominiums blossomed on the shoreline. The growing population dumped sewage into water that was already polluted by the soap local women used to wash their clothes at the lake's edge. That, coupled with political skirmishes, warring factions, and an earthquake, erased the grebe population. Disheartened, Anne LaBastille returned to the United States and cried over the bird's extinction in 1990.

Although she taught classes at various universities, lectured to diverse groups across the country, and authored an impressive list of books and articles, LaBastille preferred her work as a ecological consultant and the freedom of self-employment. She moved back to the Adirondacks and resolved to freelance. With pet German shepherds as her only permanent companions, she led a life of quiet contemplation of the beauty around her while she awaited assignments.

In 1972, LaBastille was asked to investigate the slopes of Volcan Atitlán, a volcanic peak of over eleven thousand feet in Guatemala. The government wanted to create a national park in the area, opening it to tourism, and needed to know the impact humans might have on the region's wildlife, particularly the quetzal. Considered by some to be the most beautiful bird in the world and revered by Mexican and Guatamalan Indians, who used the long, drooping tail feathers in ceremonial head dress, the quetzal dwells in tree tops and only rarely ventures out. To document the bird on film, LaBastille and her party had to construct a twenty-eight-foot observation tower in order to be at the same height as the quetzal. Eventually, it was determined that a sanctuary should be built for the birds, and a local plantation owner agreed to donate one thousand acres of land. Opened a short time later, the Biodiversity Reserve operates under the auspices of the University of the Valley in Guatamala City.

Following a brief stint in Anegada, West Indies, Anne LaBastille was contracted by the International Union for Conservation of Nature and Natural Resources in 1973 to conduct an ecological survey of Panama's first national park, Volcan Baru. In spite of strong winds on the volcanic peak, the expedition collected seventy-two specimens of plant life in and around the craters and camped on the crest longer than any other group.

One of her guides on the trek, Benjamin, was a Guaymi Indian who offered to take the expedition members to visit his native home and meet the chief. One of the more isolated groups, the Guaymi were seldom called on by outsiders and rarely by other ethnic groups. The Guaymi, anticipating the trekkers' arrival, were outfitted in their finest ceremonial dress, including a frayed tuxedo jacket donned by the chief. As the first white woman to visit the village, LaBastille was treated royally, and the chief personally decorated her face with charcoal, a red lipstick, and white clay in geometric shapes symbolizing the jaguar. The special occasion culminated in a dance resembling a conga line that she was urged to join.

On their return trip to the volcano, Benjamin lamented the inevitable assimilation of the Guaymis. The copper industry had discovered rich veins in the region and had offered to build schools for the native children and to teach them Spanish. As she listened to his sorrow, LaBastille realized that birds and wildlife were not alone on the endangered species list.

Her next assignment took her to the Dominican Republic to survey potential national park land. The trip was underwritten by Gulf + Western Industries, one of the largest corporations in the region and cultivators of sugarcane and enormous tracts of ranch land. Because funds were not in short supply, LaBastille was encouraged to tour the designated park parameters by helicopter, surveying over more than one hundred thousand acres. Once the boundaries were marked, she was invited back for a closer examination by land and recommended various reserves within the system. The Parque Nacional del Este opened in 1975 and incorporated almost two hundred thousand acres of the Dominican Republic.

Subsequent travels took her to the Amazon Basin for a three-month writing assignment in Manu National Park for *Audubon* magazine. In 1974 LaBastille was presented a Gold Medal from the World Wildlife Fund as Conservationist of the Year, citing her work with the grebes and the quetzals. From 1976 to 1993 she served as a commissioner of New York State's Adirondack Park Agency, endeavoring to protect the ecological balance of that six-million-acre tract. She is a fellow of The Explorers Club, and a member of the Society of Woman Geographers. In addition to expeditions into other regions, she continues to pen books, articles, and scientific papers and to add to her list of over four hundred lectures to Audubon clubs, universities, museums, and conservation groups.

References and Suggested Reading

LaBastille, Anne. *Jaguar Totem*. Westport, NY: West of the Wind Publications, 1999.
———. *Mama Poc*. New York: W.W. Norton Company, 1990.
———. *Woodswoman*. New York: E.P. Dutton Company, 1976.

Sharon Christa Corrigan McAuliffe
(1949–1986)

United States
Astronaut (honorary)/Educator

Although she preferred to be considered an ordinary citizen, Christa McAuliffe became extraordinary as the first civilian invited into space aboard the space shuttle *Challenger*. The beloved teacher vaulted into the spotlight as a national hero for millions of school children.

Sharon Christa Corrigan McAuliffe was born in 1949 in Farmingham, New Hampshire, the eldest of the five children of Edward and Grace Corrigan. The family was not well-to-do, living for awhile in low-income public housing, but they managed to find the funds for Christa to earn a bachelor's degree in history from Farmingham State College in 1970. After graduation she married her high school sweetheart, Steve McAuliffe, and when he completed law school, she returned to Bowie State College for a master's degree in school administration. The couple had two children and moved to Concord, where Christa taught social studies and economics classes at Concord High School. At school she was affectionately branded "The Field Trip Teacher."

In 1985 the National Aeronautics and Space Administration (NASA) sponsored a contest of sorts, seeking a civilian to ride on board the twenty-fifth flight of the space shuttle. President Ronald Reagan declared that person should be "one of America's finest, a teacher." More than eleven thousand teachers from all areas of education filled in the eleven-page application. Slowly the list was narrowed from one hundred fourteen semifinalists to ten finalists. And then there was one. Concord, New Hampshire, public school teacher Christa McAuliffe had been selected.

A somewhat dazed McAuliffe endured the press interviews, endearing herself to the reporters with her warmth, humility, and humanity. On one radio talk show, she quipped that she felt safer going up in the *Challenger* than driving around the beltway in Washington, D.C. Beneath all the bravado she worried that she would not pass the physical tests and that the other astronauts would not accept a civilian in space.

By January 28, 1986, following more than one hundred hours of intensive training, those fears were allayed and Christa McAuliffe, "teacher-naut," took her place alongside six others, including pioneering woman astronaut Judith Resnick, on the launching pad of the Kennedy Space Center. McAuliffe was scheduled to conduct two classes from space via satellite, and many school children were dismissed from classes to watch the launch.

Although the flight was designed to rekindle public excitement about the space program, few of the news media were on hand to cover the launch. The three major networks declined to interrupt regular programming, since by then shuttle flights had become rather routine news. The *Challenger* would be making its tenth flight and was known as the finest performer in the NASA fleet. It was assumed that takeoff would be as smooth as in the past.

The engines fired and the craft lifted from the pad. However, one minute into the flight and eight miles out from the Space Center, the *Challenger* exploded. For several minutes spectators on the ground and experts in the control center stared in total disbelief as the capsule burst into a whirling ball of fire and dived into the sea. A malfunction had caused the external fuel tank to detonate, marking the first major disaster in fifty-six manned space missions and burying all those on board in water seventy to two hundred feet deep.

Christa McAuliffe was no ordinary woman. The entire world mourned her loss, and a whole generation asked the question, "Where were you when the *Challenger* exploded?" In 1990 the Christa McAuliffe Planetarium opened in New Hampshire, and each year some thirty thousand school children tour the facility on "the ultimate field trip." McAuliffe continues to teach.

References and Suggested Reading

Corrigan, Grace George. *A Journal for Christa*. Lincoln: University of Nebraska Press, 1993.

Hohler, Robert. *I Touch the Future: The Story of Christa McAuliffe*. New York: Random House, 1986.

Life (obituary) (March 1986) 9: 8.

Richman, Alan. "A Lesson in Uncommon Valor." *People's Weekly*, 10 February 1986, 25: 32–36.

Van Biema, David H. "Christa McAuliffe Gets NASA's Nod to Conduct America's First Classroom in Space." *People's Weekly*, 5 August 1985, 24: 28–32.

Beryl Clutterbuck Markham
(1902–1986)

England
Aviator

Courtesy of the Library of Congress

Licensed race horse trainer and breeder, commercial pilot, and elephant scout, Beryl Markham was, in a word, unconventional. She was one of the pioneers in women's aviation, earning part of her living as a bush pilot in Africa.

Although she was born in Leicester, England, in 1902, Beryl Markham spent most of her life in Africa. When her mother, Clara Alexander, abandoned her at age four, Markham's father, Charles B. Clutterbuck, a scholar and adventurer, took the young girl to British East Africa. There he purchased a farm in Njora, seventy miles from Nairobi, and soon discovered he was not cut from agrarian cloth. He did, however, begin a profitable trade in breeding race horses for the Nairobi tracks and trained his daughter to work with the animals.

As a child Beryl spent time with the local Murani chieftain, learning to hunt and ride and playing with his son. Her early adventures included a confrontation with a lion and killing a poisonous black mamba snake. Although she was briefly expelled from the Nairobi school for trying to cause a "revolt," she easily mastered the Swahili, Nandi, and Masai languages, which would later ease her entrance into business dealings with the natives.

Shortly after her father presented her with her own horse, named "Pegasus," an oppressive drought hit the region, eventually causing him to lose the farm. He left for better opportunities in Peru, and although he asked his seventeen-year-old daughter to accompany him, she opted to stay behind. Left to her own devices, Beryl worked for a horse trainer's license, which she earned at eighteen, the first woman in Africa to achieve that distinction.

Her career path soon took a sharp turn away from involvement with horses, with the exception, perhaps, of the original Pegasus. Noted big game hunter and friend, Denys Finch Hatton, took her up for a short flight in his plane. Markham wanted to learn to fly but that ambition was put on hold for a short time, interrupted by a brief marriage to wealthy Englishman Mansfield Markham in 1927, relocation with him to England, and the subsequent birth of their son, Gervase.

By the early 1930s Beryl was back in Africa, newly divorced, and ready to learn to fly. In only eighteen months she logged over one thousand hours of flight time and gained a commercial pilot's license, the first license of the type awarded to a woman in Kenya. She was required to pass a grueling written math test as well take apart and reassemble an aircraft engine.

Due in part to her financial circumstances and in part to her gritty determination, Markham needed to make flight more than a diversion. For several years she worked as a bush pilot flying mail, passengers, medicine, and supples to isolated mining settlements and hunters' camps in East Africa. Many of those outposts were remote, and she became skilled at locating "landing strips" among the clearings and fields. She also picked up extra income by inventing big game hunting by air, scouting and locating large herds and dropping her passengers as close as possible to their quarry.

By 1936 Beryl Markham had covered a quarter of a million miles in her air travels and decided she was up for a challenge—crossing the Atlantic from England to New York. She flew "west with the night," the title of her autobiography, through nineteen hours of darkness and a raging rain storm. The plane was sighted over Ireland, the Atlantic, and Newfoundland but then disappeared; with no radio on board, all contact was lost. But Markham was not. Over Nova Scotia the engine spluttered because of a frozen fuel line, and the plane went down, nose first in a muddy peat bog on Cape Breton Island. With her usual aplomb Beryl climbed out of the cockpit and was instantly mired in ooze up to her knees. She looked at her watch. In spite of not making it to New York as planned, she had made the flight in twenty-two hours and twenty-five minutes, a first for women fliers. She was transported to New York City by land, hailed as a hero, shook the hand of Mayor Fiorello La-Guardia, and given a ticker-tape parade through the city. Offers poured in, including a tempting one from a Hollywood talent scout, but Markham failed the screen test arranged for her.

Beryl Markham moved to the United States in 1939 for a short period, where she remarried and ran a California avocado ranch. When that marriage failed, she tried yet a third time, wedding Raoul Schumacher, a writer. She worked on her memoirs during her time with Schumacher and published *West with the Night* in 1942. Marriage was not her long suit, however, and at fifty, finding herself alone once again, perhaps a condition she preferred, Markham borrowed money, returned to Africa, and purchased a ranch. From 1958 to 1972 she was the most successful horse trainer in Kenya with her stable winning all the major races.

In the mid-1980s there was a resurgence of interest in Markham's life, producing a ten-hour documentary on Public Broadcasting Stations, feature films and a republication of her autobiography, which sold one hundred forty thousand copies. In 1986 at age eighty-one, still sharp-tongued and hard drinking, she died in Nairobi, Kenya.

After her death the facts and myths of her personal life were in the news again when her third husband, Raoul Schumacher, claimed that Markham was barely literate and he was the actual author of *West with the Night*. Although his assertion was discredited, other facets of Markham's past resurfaced. It was rumored that she had had relationships with the writer Antoine de Saint-Exupery and musical conductor Leo-pold Stokowski, that she had run barefoot through Buckingham Palace with Prince Henry, that she always took her twin bull dogs to formal dinners, and that she doctored her horses with herbal potions given to her by African healers. None of the rumors were substantiated but they did serve to build a large demand for written and visual materials on the independent spirit that was Beryl Markham.

References and Suggested Reading

Leicester, Overseas Web site. "Beryl Markham." *http://www.Leicesteroverseas.com/Beryl_Markham.htm*
Lovell, Mary S. *Straight on Till Morning.* New York: St. Martin's Press, 1987.
Time (obituary). 18 August 1986, 128: 70.

Margaret Mead
(1901–1979)

United States
Anthropologist

Courtesy of the Library of Congress

Often considered an enigma in her personal life and a perfection-ist professionally, Margaret Mead combined the fields of an-thropology and psychology to illustrate the effects of the cultural milieu on personality. She was one of the first to make anthro-pology accessible to the layman and to demonstrate its importance to the general population.

Margaret Mead was born in Philadelphia, the eldest child of academic parents. Her father, Edward Sherwood Mead, was a professor of eco-nomics at the University of Pennsylvania, and her mother, Emily Fogg Mead, was a sociologist, a feminist, and a suffragist. The young woman received her primary education at home from her grandmother, a retired teacher, who trained her to be a social scientist, even though Margaret was more interested in painting.

After a short trial as an English major at DePauw University in 1919, she transferred to Barnard College, earning her bachelor's degree in 1923. From there she entered Columbia University in New York City and stud-ied under the famed anthropologist Franz Boas, who peaked her interest in that discipline and added to her growing interest in psychology. Boaz's assistant at the time was Ruth Benedict, who became a mentor and life-long friend to Mead. After earning a master's degree from Co-lumbia in 1924 in psychology and being inducted into Phi Beta Kappa, Mead enrolled in the doctoral program and was married, briefly, to Lu-ther Cresswell, an archaeoanthropologist. She was awarded a National Research Council Fellowship, which allowed her to travel to the Bishop Museum in Honolulu and from there to Samoa for primary research.

The predominant part of her theory of personality was formulated during her year-long sojourn in Samoa. She posited that cultural con-ditioning, not genetics, molded human behavior, a theory that came to be called cultural determinism. Although she was often criticized for relying on observation rather than statistical sampling to gather data, it was her research during that period that highlighted her career, secured her place in history, and created the best-selling *Coming of Age in Samoa* (1928). A pivotal work that opened the field of anthropology to a general reading audience while shocking many of Mead's colleagues, the book examined gender roles, rites of passage, and sexual practices among the Samoans. In later years much of her research was attacked as unverifi-able by some in her field, particularly by her competitor, anthropologist Derek Freeman, but others defended her thesis and accepted her findings as inviolate.

In 1926, with doctorate in hand, Margaret Mead accepted a position with the Department of Anthropology at the American Museum of Natural History, an appointment she held until her death. She was largely responsible for gathering the artifacts included in the museum's Hall of Pacific Peoples. To enrich the collection as well as add to the research on populations, Mead made numerous expeditions into the Pacific Islands, including treks into New Guinea and Bali. Mead was an innovator in technique, employing film and photography to document her studies. In addition, she was one of the first in her field to include child rearing as a cultural ingredient and to conduct pioneering studies on generational links and gender roles, recording the status of women in a number of cultures. In all of her field work she assumed the same role that was prescribed for the native women to avoid cultural divergence and the imposition of her mores on the group under study.

During her sojourns in the field, Margaret Mead's personal life was as multicultural as her professional one. She married twice more during this period, each time to a fellow anthropologist, one from New Zealand and one from England. She wed her second husband, Reo Fortune, on board ship en route to investigate the Melanesian peoples of Manus Island in the Admiralty chain. In 1932 they worked together on an exhaustive analysis of western Native Americans. She met her third husband, Gregory Bateson, the father of her only child Mary Catherine, as an associate in New Guinea. They later worked together on Bali.

Although she was best known for her work with the nonliterate peoples of Oceania, Mead scrutinized her own society during World War II in an effort to mend cultural lesions between the United States and Britain. She taught classes at Vassar College in 1939, was director of Columbia University Research in Contemporary Cultures in 1948, and an adjunct professor at that institution in 1954.

In addition to her exhaustive studies of island societies, Mead gained a solid domestic reputation as an outspoken activist for a variety of causes from nuclear proliferation to the legalization of marijuana, from population control to sexual morality, and from race relations to environmental pollution. She testified before the United States Congress on numerous occasions, addressing many of those issues. By sheer force of will Mead made her own rules as she went along. She was a firm believer in networking, and in her own way created extended families among the vast varieties of people she encountered during her journey through life. She was a champion of women's rights, becoming a mentor and protector and offering empowerment or employment to a host of troubled persons who sought her out.

From the mid-1940s until her death, Margaret Mead collaborated on projects across a wide range of academic and scientific subjects and was particularly interested in the merging of anthropology and psychiatry. She was at her best in interdisciplinary conferences, and she participated in an array of organizations from the World Council of Churches to the New Alchemists. She received twenty-eight honorary degrees, was elected to the National Academy of Sciences, and appointed president of the American Association for the Advancement of Science (AAAS) in 1976.

In 1978 Margaret Mead died of cancer, the only facet of her life over which she had no control. She was posthumously awarded the Presidential Medal of Freedom, the highest civilian honor given by the United States government.

References and Suggested Reading

Bateson, Mary Catherine. *With a Daughter's Eye: A Memoir of Margaret Mead and Gregory Bateson*. New York: Morrow, 1984. Reprint 1994.

Foerstal, Lenora, and Angela Gilliam. *Confronting the Margaret Mead Legacy: Scholarship, Empire and the South Pacific*. Philadelphia: Temple University Press, 1994.

Goode, Stephen. "The Decline and Fall of Anthropology." *Insight on the News*, 15 March 1993, 9: 12–18.

Howard, Jane. *Margaret Mead, a Life*. New York: Simon and Schuster, 1984. Reprint 1990.

"Margaret Mead: A Pioneer in Anthropology." *Monkeyshines on Health and Science* (Fall 1995): 32–33.

Sylvia Earle Mead
(1935–   )

United States
Aquanaut/Oceanographer

S ylvia Earle has led more than fifty expeditions worldwide and spent six thousand hours underwater. Among innumerable other honors, including being recognized by the Library of Congress as a living legend, she headed the first all-woman team to reside for an extended period of time on the ocean floor.

Sylvia Earle was born in Gibbstown, New Jersey, in 1935. Her father, Lewis Reade Earle, an electrical contractor, and her mother, Alice Freas Richie, a nurse, moved the family to Florida in the early 1950s. While studying botany at Florida State University, Sylvia learned to scuba dive in the Gulf of Mexico, a haven of blue and green that would eventually encompass her world.

After earning a bachelor's degree from Florida State and a doctorate from Duke University in North Carolina, Earle worked for the United States Fish and Wildlife Bureau in Beaufort, North Carolina, as a fisheries biologist. When that position failed to provide enough hours in the water to suit her, she joined the International Indian Ocean Expedition as a diver, the only woman among sixty men on that long-term operation. Returning to Florida when the expedition had successfully completed its assignment, Sylvia became the director of the Mote Marine Lab, where she supervised one hundred scientists involved in ecological and environmental studies. While working at the lab, she met and married ichthyologist Giles Mead, then at Harvard University. She resigned her position and moved with Mead to Cambridge, Massachusetts, where she conducted research at the Radcliffe Institute and supervised the Man-in-Sea Project in the Bahamas in 1968 under the auspices of the Smithsonian Institute. During that period she was certified to dive to fifty meters and subsequently became the first person of either gender to solo dive to one thousand meters.

By the late 1960s, the *Tektite II* experiment, funded and monitored by the National Aeronautics and Space Administration (NASA), was underway. *Tektite II* is a sustainable underwater laboratory that can house scientists for weeks at a time. NASA concluded that experimentation on biofeedback below the surface could be successfully generalized to life in space and manned the capsule to research the effects of deprivation on the human body. For several years only men had worked in the submerged living quarters in Great Lameshur Bay off the Virgin Islands, but in 1970 Sylvia Earle was asked to lead the first all-woman team, labeled "Aquanauts," to live in the ocean.

For a two-week period the five women spent from six to ten hours each day outside their capsule and together they logged more than one thousand hours exploring their environs with the aid of scuba gear. During their second day in their temporary home, an earthquake rumbled across the ocean floor, but there was little damage to the vehicle or personnel. Later, they discovered that their salty laboratory was situated close to the earthquake's epicenter and realized how fortunate they had been. In their time spent outside the lab, the divers observed thirty-five species of fish and one hundred fifty-four varieties of marine plants, twenty-six of which had never been seen in that area before.

When the two weeks were completed, the women were squeezed into a decompression chamber for twenty hours to allow their systems to readjust to life on land. Afterwards, they were feted with lunch at the White House, presented the Conservation Service Award, and were in the world media spotlight for a short time. Sylvia considered all the attention a type of reverse discrimination, since the men who went before as residents on the *Tektite II* had hardly received notice.

Always concerned with the interrelationship of marine plants and animals and with ocean pollution, Sylvia Earle spent the next twenty years diving in various parts of the world. From the Gulf of Mexico to the Indian Ocean and the Pacific, where she led an expedition to the Galapagos Islands in 1972, she created public awareness of the importance of sea exploration. She wrote more than one hundred articles on marine science, authored the book *Sea Change* (1995), and held honorary doctorates from eleven colleges and universities.

From 1980 to 1984 Earle was a member of the President's Advisory Committee on Oceans and Atmosphere and was appointed chief scientist of the National Oceanic and Atmospheric Administration (NOAA), where she served until 1992.

In addition to being explorer in residence of the National Geographic Society and honorary president of the Explorers Club, Earle founded an undersea systems integration firm in 1992. The DOER (Deep Ocean Exploration and Research) firm designs and operates robotic systems, known as remotely operated vehicles (ROV). Contracted by *National Geographic*, DOER, with Sylvia Earle as leader, conducted the Sustainable Seas Expedition, a five-year study of national marine sanctuaries. In addition, she created a series of documentaries to draw attention to the national marine underwater park system.

References and Suggested Reading

Academy of Achievement Web site. "Sylvia Earle." *http://www.achievement.org/autodoc/page/ear0int-1*

Divernet Web site. A Visit from Aquababe Number One." *http://www.divernet.co.uk/profs/earl1196.htm*

DOER Inc. Web site. *http://www.doer-INC.com*
Earle, Sylvia H. "All-Girl Team Tests the Habitat." *National Geographic* (August 1971): 291.
SeaWeb Web site. *www.seaweb.org*

Ruth Nichols
(1901–1960)

United States
Aviator

Courtesy of the Library of Congress

K nown for her dogged perseverance, Ruth Nichols held more than thirty-five "firsts" in aviation and survived six major accidents. Were it not for one of those mishaps, she would likely have been the first woman pilot to cross the North Atlantic.

Ruth Nichols was born into a wealthy family in 1901 in New York City. Her father, Erickson Norman Nichols, was a stockbroker and at one time a member of Teddy Roosevelt's Rough Riders. Edith Corlis Haines Nichols, Ruth's mother, was a Quaker with well-defined opinions on the appropriate behavior for a young woman ready to assume her place in society.

Ruth's ideas about what was acceptable changed markedly in 1919 when her father took her to an air show as a high school graduation present. Fascinated by the planes and the fliers, she was permitted to go up for a ten-minute romp over Atlantic City, New Jersey, in a plane piloted by World War I ace Eddie Stinson. In her autobiography, *Wings for Life* (1957), Nichols proclaimed that she had not "come down to earth since."

Postponing her mother's wish to present her to society at a debutante ball, Nichols enrolled at Wellesley College in the premedical program. During a school break she joined her family on holiday in Miami where she met Harry Rogers, barnstormer and pilot of a "flying boat," as seaplanes were called. He took her up for a ride, allowed her to hold the controls of the plane, and was persuaded to become her teacher, a fact she chose not to share with her parents.

In 1927 Nichols received her degree from Wellesley and her international hydroplane license, the first woman in the world to do so. She weighed her two options, medical school or aviation, but her parents discouraged both. To appease them, she briefly took a position in a New York City bank. She continued to take flying lessons, however, and became one of the first two women awarded a transport license from the Department of Commerce.

She was rescued from the dreary world of high finance on New Year's Eve in 1927 when her mentor, Harry Rogers, asked her to co-pilot a nonstop flight from New York to Miami. Nichols jumped at the chance. The junket was completed in a record-setting twelve hours and, as others of her day, Ruth Nichols was elevated to national stardom, primarily by virtue of being a woman in a man's domain. As a result of media coverage and name recognition, she was offered a job in sales promotion with Fairchild Airplane and Engine Company, which she accepted.

During 1928 Nichols tried to establish a nationwide chain of aviation country clubs, a membership-only social group whose goal was to participate in and champion the joys of flying. After establishing the first club in Hicksville, Long Island, she flew to forty-six states promoting the venture. Others appeared ready to join until the stock market crash of 1929 curtailed their enthusiasm for spending investment capitol.

Dressed in her custom-made purple leather flight suit and purple helmet, Ruth Nichols spent the early part of 1931 breaking aviation records. She set a new time for a transcontinental flight in both directions, east to west and west to east, and then sought the prize for altitude. The craft she was piloting had no on-board oxygen system; thus, Nichols loaded on a compressed oxygen tank equipped with a rubber hose from which she drew air straight into her mouth. Unfortunately, she had overlooked a basic principle of chemistry—gas assumes the temperature of the air around it. At twenty thousand feet the oxygen she inhaled was 60 degrees below zero, causing her tongue to go completely numb. She succeeded in setting a new altitude record for women at 28,743 feet, which left her speechless, her rather blue tongue temporarily incapable of forming words.

By summer she was ready to soar across the Atlantic, but on her first refueling stop in New Brunswick, she overshot the runway and smashed into a hillside. She cracked five vertebrae and her doctors grounded her for a year. The doctors, however, were unaccustomed to Ruth Nichols's brand of persistence, and by the end of the month after the crash, she drove her car for thirteen consecutive hours to prove she could undertake the transatlantic jaunt. Two months after the accident, still encased in plaster, she was ready to fly.

Fall approached and Nichols readied for the crossing, but for twenty-five consecutive days, torrential rains plummeted down on Paris, her final destination. Postponing her takeoff once again, Ruth sought a different record to break. In October, wearing a steel corset brace, she boarded her aircraft in California for a nonstop run to New York. However, just outside of Chicago an impenetrable fog obscured her path, and she had to abandon the flight at the nearest airport, Louisville, Kentucky. She had still set a distance record for women. The next day, as she was preparing for takeoff, a spark from the plane's exhaust ignited fuel from a leaky valve and set the vehicle on fire. Nichols managed to crawl out of the craft moments before it exploded. The crisis put an indefinite hold on her transatlantic plans, and while she negotiated for a new plane, her friend Amelia Earhart became the first woman to fly across the Atlantic.

In 1932 Ruth made a goodwill tour in support of the International Congress of Women, and the next year she completed her New York to Los Angeles record-setting run, dropping campaign literature for Herbert Hoover en route.

Returning to New York, Nichols was determined to raise funds for a round-the-world attempt. To that end she accepted an offer from Clarence Chamberlin to co-pilot a transport plane on a barnstorming tour of New England. At Troy, New York, the aircraft made an emergency landing, missed the runway completely, and caught on fire. Nichols was thrown out, critically injured, and forced to recuperate for two years. Grounded, she went to work for the Emergency Peace Campaign, a pacifist Quaker organization in Philadelphia, to warn about the dangers of international conflicts.

At the advent of World War II, the aviator launched Relief Wings, a civilian air ambulance service that was officially inaugurated in 1940. By the following year there were centers in thirty-six states, and when the United States joined the battle, Nichols turned over the assets to the Civil Air Patrol. She served as a volunteer Red Cross nurse's aide and gave flying lessons during the war.

With Amelia Earhart, she co-founded the Ninety-Nines, an international organization of women fliers, and was instrumental in involving women in all areas of aviation. She piloted a world tour for the United Nations International Children's Emergency Fund (UNICEF), served as an adviser to the national commander on aeromedical administration for the Civil Air Patrol, and in 1955 became the first woman to fly a twin engine jet, setting speed and altitude records in the process.

In 1960, Ruth Nichols was found in her New York apartment, the victim of an apparent suicide.

References and Suggested Reading

Harris, Sherwood. *The First to Fly: Aviation's Pioneer Days*. New York: Simon and Schuster, 1970.
Jablonski, Edward. *Ladybirds: Women in Aviation*. Hawthorn Books, 1968.
Nichols, Ruth. *Wings for Life*. New York: Lippincott, 1957.

Valentina Tereshkova Nikolayev
(1937–)

Russian
Cosmonaut

Courtesy of C. L. Osborne

Although she had no formal training in astrophysics or previous experience as a pilot, Valentina Nikolayev became the first woman in space in 1963. After orbiting the earth forty-eight times, she was lauded as a symbol of the New Soviet Woman.

Valentina Tereshkova Nikolayev was born in 1937 on a farm in the village of Maslennikovo on the Volga River. Her father, Vladimir, was a tractor driver, and a fatality of World War II. Her mother, Elena Fyodorovna, worked in a cotton mill. When Valentina was a child, the family was impoverished and she could not afford to begin school until she was ten years old. At seventeen she began working at the Yaroslavl Tire Factory, taking night classes when she could. Eventually, she joined her mother in the textile factory and became an active member of Comsomol, the Young Communists League. In 1959 Nikolayev joined the Yaroslavl Air Sports Club, where she learned parachute jumping. She received a first-class certificate of proficiency after only one year.

In 1961 an event occurred that altered Valentina's path and mapped the route that would propel her into international fame. That year Russian cosmonaut Yuri Gagarin became the first person to travel into outer space. Inspired by his success and intrigued by the possibilities, she volunteered for the space program and was accepted.

After joining the Communist party in 1962 as one of the youngest members in the Soviet Union, Nikolayev trained for space travel for a full year, often astounding her male counterparts with her physical endurance and stamina. In June 1963 she became the first woman in space. The *Vostok VI* completed forty-eight orbits, traveling 1.2 million miles in three days. At speeds of eighteen thousand miles per hour, the vehicle circled the earth every 88.3 minutes. Early space vehicles had no landing capability; thus, at the end of the flight, Valentina had to eject from the craft and parachute back to earth.

She was celebrated internationally, officially declared a hero of the Soviet Union, and awarded the Order of Lenin and the Gold Star. Premier Nikita Khrushchev shook her hand and proclaimed woman as the weaker sex a myth, since this cosmonaut had been in orbit longer than all of her American male counterparts combined.

In a second media blitz Valentina married fellow cosmonaut Andrian Nikolayev shortly after her flight. Some critics felt the marriage was arranged by the government as a means of promotion, which may have been true since the union was short-lived.

After her historic flight Valentina served as an ambassador of goodwill for the Soviet government, advocating for such issues as broader international cooperation and women's rights.

References and Suggested Reading

"Coloring the Cosmos Pink." *Time*, 13 June 1983, 121: 58–59.
O'Neill, Bill. "Whatever Became of Valentina Tereshkova?" *New Scientist*, 14 August 1993, 139: 21–24.

Marianne North
(1830–1890)

→

England
Conservationist/Explorer

Reserved and cautious in her dealings with people, Marianne North preferred to spend her time with the flora of the world, preserving species in over eight hundred paintings. She went around the world twice, touring five continents in a span of twenty years.

Marianne North was born in 1830 in Hastings, England. Her father, Frederick, was the idol of her life, and her first memories were of riding on his shoulders along Hastings Beach. Her education came primarily from independent reading and leisurely travel with her family, creating a childhood altogether carefree and unfettered. North's mother died in 1855, and the young woman became her father's constant companion, traveling with him throughout Europe and into parts of Asia. When Frederick died in 1869, Marianne was alone for the first time in her life, and although she had been exposed to society, she had never faced people without her father at her side.

At forty-one she began traveling alone, an undertaking she considered not pleasure but work. She was attracted to the sciences early on, and even had casual friendships with Charles Darwin and others in the scientific community but she was also aware that women were not taken seriously as scientists. One area of science, however, did permit distaff membership, and that was botany. Women, it was assumed, should like flowers, and everyone needed a hobby.

Over the twenty-year span of her pilgrimage, North visited Syria, the Nile, North America, the West Indies, Brazil, Japan, Borneo, Java, Singapore, Sri Lanka, India, and South Africa. From barren plains to mountain forests, she traveled alone, often on muleback, moving from one jungle hut to another. Along the way she painted hundreds of flowers.

Her first trip was to Canada, the United States, and Jamaica. Traveling on to Brazil, she toured gold mines accessible only by mule train through drenching rains and slippery mud. Along the way she examined the plant life, discovering some previously unidentified varieties and drawing each in an accurate, scientific manner.

In 1875 she joined a tour en route to Japan via Canada and the United States. The group journeyed from Quebec to Salt Lake City, where she shook the hand of Mormon leader, Brigham Young, whom she found to be an "old wretch." Always uncomfortable in company, she escaped the tour and traveled alone into California, arriving in the land of the giant redwoods, where she regained personal harmony. Back on the tour, North surveyed Java by cart and horseback, learned to speak the Malay dialect, and climbed to the top of volcanic peaks.

Becoming obsessed with painting, Marianne raced across India in 1877, where she studied temples and wandered among the foothills of the Himalayas. During part of that junket, she traveled in a litter held precariously on the heads of her native bearers. She had little use for the population of that or any culture, may have held racist beliefs, and wasted none of her years in sociological or anthropological studies. It was the flowers that concerned her, and she apparently liked them much better than people.

In 1882 she funded a gallery at Kew Botanical Gardens to hold her paintings, works that she and the majority of critics did not consider art, but scientific illustrations. North supervised construction of the rooms, framed and hung the work herself, and stenciled the walls. Eight hundred paintings, in oil on cardboard, were on display for the opening. An explosion of gaudy, many-hued flowers and ferns and trees and fungi represented twenty years of Marianne North's life. The tightly packed paintings, a botanist's surreal nightmare, featured artistic perspective similar to North's personal perspective—oversized flora dwarfed minuscule gray people.

Wanting to have the collection truly represent all areas of the Earth, she ventured out again in 1880, touring Australia (which she liked for its underpopulation), New Zealand, and Hawaii, then back to the United States mainland for a return visit with her old friends, the redwoods of California. Only one continent with vegetation was left, and North arrived in Cape Town, South Africa in 1882. Her sojourn there was rather abrupt, however, for she was becoming increasingly deaf and suffered from "nerves," which produced a certain paranoia.

Retiring to her home in Gloucestershire with a garden featuring transplanted species from all over the world, North began work on her memoirs, *Recollections of a Happy Life* and *Further Recollections*. It was likely that she suffered from mental illness near the end of her life and often complained of seeing things not there and of hearing voices in her head. Her sister, Catherine, Mrs. Addington Symonds, attributed Marianne's delusions to bad food or a biproduct of her deafness. North died before completing her manuscripts, but her sister edited the material and secured a publisher. One variety of the capuchin tree, which she liked almost as much as the redwoods, was renamed Northea in her honor.

References and Suggested Reading

Losano, Antonia. "A Preference for Vegetables: The Travel Writings and Botanical Art of Marianne North." *Women's Studies* (October 1997) 26: 423–449.

Macksey, Joan, and Kenneth Macksey. *The Guinness Guide to Feminine Achievement*. Enfield, England: Guinness Superlatives, Ltd., 1975.

Shteir, Ann B. *Cultivating Women, Cultivating Science: Flora's Daughters and Botany in England 1760–1860*. Baltimore: The Johns Hopkins University Press, 1996.

"A Vision of Eden." *Ms. Magazine* (July 1986): 27.

Diana Sneed Nyad
(1949–   )

United States
Marathon Swimmer

For a decade Diana Nyad held the record as the best marathoner in the world for both distance and speed. Best remembered of those feats was a harrowing two-day marathon from the Bahama Islands to Florida in 1979.

Diana Sneed Nyad was born in New York City in 1949 to stockbroker William Sneed and his wife, Lucy Curtis. Her father died when she was an infant, and when she was three, her mother married Aristotle Nyad, a Greek land developer, who adopted the young child. The family moved to Fort Lauderdale, Florida, and Diana began serious swimming when she was in the seventh grade.

In addition to swimming, Nyad was also a squash champion, and once ranked thirteenth among women nationally. She practiced both sports with the hope of competing in the Mexico City Olympics in 1968, but that hope was dashed when she contracted endocarditis, a viral infection of the heart, and was prescribed a year of rest. In 1967 she enrolled in the premedical program at Emory University but was expelled after parachuting out of her dormitory window. She spent a year traveling, life guarding, and waitressing before returning to academia. In 1970 she earned a bachelor's degree in both English and French from Lake Forest College in Illinois and was inducted into Phi Beta Kappa.

Shortly after graduation Nyad began training to swim marathons. Her first major undertaking was the ten-mile crossing of Lake Ontario, setting the women's time record. In 1970 she won the women's world marathon record and over the next five years broke innumerable records, swimming between twenty-two and fifty miles in such diverse bodies of water as the Suez Canal, the North Sea, the Nile, and the Caribbean. During this time she dried off long enough for postgraduate work at New York University in comparative literature.

Needing to add another record to her growing list, Diana Nyad resolved to be the first person to swim from the Caribbean Islands to Florida. However, her initial attempt in 1978 from Cuba had to be aborted. The waters were notoriously shark-infested; consequently, she had to splash through the one hundred and three miles of surf encased in a cumbersome metal shark cage. Although the cage offered protection from sharks, it did not deter a Portuguese man-of-war, and Nyad had to abandon her quest after she was stung.

The next year the marathoner tried the waters again, this time departing from North Bimini Island in the Bahamas. She successfully navigated the eighty-nine miles to Juno Beach, Florida, in the water for twenty-seven and one-half hours. The swim established a record for both men and women that was not broken until 1997. Nyad was inducted into the National Women's Sports Hall of Fame in 1986.

Turning to journalism in 1991, Diana Nyad was successively a studio anchor for the USA Network, covering the U.S. Open Tennis Tournament; senior correspondent at Fox Sports TV in 1999; Outdoor Life Network special reporter on world wildlife; and columnist for National Public Radio's (NPR) "Morning Edition."

References and Suggested Reading

"Diana Nyad Heads for the Aegean." *Newsweek*, 25 February 1980: 10.
Greenspan, Emily. "Out of the Water and Onto the Airwaves." *Ms. Magazine* (March 1985): 74.
Nyad, Diana. *Other Shores*. New York: Random House, 1978.

Annie Smith Peck
(1850–1935)

United States
Mountaineer

Courtesy of the Library of Congress

In a *New York Times* obituary Annie Smith Peck was called "the most famous of all women mountain climbers." By ascending stratospheric peaks in Peru, the former academic set the American altitude record for women in the Western Hemisphere.

Annie Smith Peck was born in 1850 in Providence, Rhode Island. She was the daughter of George Bachelor Peck, an attorney and legislator, and Ann Power Smith. As a child Annie was in constant competition with her three older brothers, who felt the little girl should be excluded from boy's play. That early exclusion might have been instrumental in her later activism as a suffragist and ardent feminist.

She read the classics at the University of Michigan and earned a bachelor's degree in Greek in 1878, followed by a master's in 1881. From 1881 to 1883 she taught at Purdue University in Indiana, one of the first women in America given the rank of college professor. Traveling to Europe in 1885, she studied German and music in Hanover and later that year was the first woman admitted to the American School of Classical Studies in Athens, Greece. While on a school holiday in Switzerland, she was intrigued by the Matterhorn and silently promised herself that she would conquer that peak someday.

After returning to the United States Peck taught Latin at Smith College, but recalling her promise to herself, she trained to climb mountains. Her first ascent was California's Mount Shasta in 1888. In 1895 she kept the promise to herself. At forty-five years of age and in knickers, a tunic, and a felt hat tied on with a veil, she became one of only three women in the nineteenth century to crest the Matterhorn. She was the only one of the three to do so in pants.

Peck gave up teaching to join the lecture circuit, traveling the United States to talk about her exploits. Labeled, even then, as the "Queen of the Climbers," she was popular and marketable; in fact, the Singer Manufacturing Company inserted one of her photographs into the package with every new machine as a promotional gimmick.

In 1897 she climbed the Jungfrau in Switzerland and Popocatépetl and Orizaba in Mexico. The latter is the third highest summit in North America and the highest altitude reached by a woman at that time. To underscore the scientific nature of her exploits, Peck took along a mercurial barometer to measure the altitude accurately.

She founded the American Alpine Club with others in 1902 and the next year attempted the first ascent of Mount Sorata in Bolivia, a height of 20,500 feet. Peck mounted the expedition with a professor whom she barely knew but who had asked to come along. Partway up the mountain, he refused to continue, and encouraged by his indifference, the native porters went on strike. Annie canceled the climb. A few months later, she made another attempt with much the same results; at one point she turned around and the porters had vanished. If this fearless, "most famous of all women mountain climbers" had a fault, it was her trusting nature. She was a poor judge of character. Giving up Sorata, Peck eyed Peru and Huascaran.

Getting there was half the fun. Over a four-week period, funded in part by *Harper's* magazine, Annie plowed through areas rife with yellow fever and bubonic plague, traveling on steamers and small boats. When she reached one destination, there was no harbor and she had to be passed from hand to hand in a barrel to reach land. From there she traveled by rail to Lake Titicaca, the world's highest lake, a journey that took her from sea level to 14,600 feet in sixty hours. A carriage ride to La Paz followed. At last she reached the base of Huascaran, the highest point in the Peruvian Andes.

She attempted the ascent five times and failed, but on the sixth she became the highest American in the Western Hemisphere. Nearly sixty years old, wearing a woolen face mask with a moustache painted on and an anorak or Eskimo suit borrowed from the Museum of Natural History, Peck almost scampered up the icy, gale-swept face of the mountain. One of her guides commented that she went where a chipmunk could not go, and he had not believed they would get out alive, particularly since she chose to make the descent at night.

On the way up one of the porters had irretrievably dropped her trusty barometer, and she could only guess at the altitude. Her estimate was twenty-four thousand feet, which would make the climb a world's altitude record for women. Others, particularly her rival Fanny Bullock Workman, disagreed. Workman hired her own team of experts to fly to Peru and triangulate the mountain, proving it only 21,812, and allowing Fanny to retain the title of highest altitude reached by a woman climber via her ascent of 23,300-foot Nun Kun peak in 1906.

The journey and the ascent proving quite enough excitement for a bit, Annie plotted her return along a less exacting route, across the Pampa of Islay and through the desert. The government of Peru awarded her a gold medal and she addressed the Lima Geographical Society, the first woman to do so in Spanish. In 1911, at age sixty-one, Peck climbed Mount Coropuna in Peru, planting a "Votes for Women" sign on the summit, and returned to the Andes several times between 1922 and 1924. She published *A Search for the Apex of America* (1911) and *The South American Tour* (1913) chronicling her adventures. In 1928 the Lima Geographical Society renamed Huascaran's north peak *Cumbre Ana Peck* in her honor.

Peck's next excursion into South America was by plane in 1929. Taking seven months, she flew over and around the country, from Panama to Tierra del Fuego, on primitive aircraft. Ironically, the plane's altitude never exceeded the height she had reached on foot. Her impressions of the trip were recorded in *Flying Over South America: 20,000 Miles by Air* (1932), published with the hope of improving inter-American relations.

Her last ascent, at age eighty-two, was Mount Madison in New Hampshire, and two years later, she boarded a cruise ship to the West Indies and Trinidad, traveling alone. In 1935 Peck departed for a seventy-five-day world tour but turned back due to failing health. She died that year in New York City.

References and Suggested Reading

Adelman, Joseph. *Famous Women*. New York: Ellis Lonow Company, 1926.
Buck, Daniel. "Road Writers: Venturing to the Far Corners of South America." *Americas* (January/February 1998) 50: 14–22.
Olds, Elizabeth Fagg. *Women of the Four Winds*. Boston: Houghton Mifflin, 1985.
Robinson, Charles Turek. "Peck's Bad Girl." *Yankee* (February 1997) 61: 86–90.
Tinling, Marion. *Women into the Unknown: A Sourcebook on Women Explorers and Travellers*. Westport, CT: Greenwood Press, 1989.

Harriet Quimby
(1875–1912)

United States
Aviator

Courtesy of Mary Quimby

I n 1910, when aviation was only nine years old and only seven years after the Wright brother's historic puddle jump in Kitty Hawk, respected journalist Harriet Quimby wanted to learn to fly. Taking lessons in secret to avoid the scrutiny of her peers in the press, she became the first licensed woman pilot in the United States and the second in the world.

Harriet Quimby was born in Coldwater, Michigan, in 1875. Failing as a farmer, her father, William, moved the family west and opened an unsuccessful grocery store in Arroyo Grande, one hundred miles north of Santa Barbara. Her mother, Ursula, rescued the family from starvation by concocting and marketing herbal medicines and by sewing sacks for prunes for a local fruit-packing factory. A determined woman, Ursula resolved to make a better life for her two daughters and weaved a fantasy about wealth, familial connections, and classic educations around the girls, primarily to encourage acceptable suitors.

Not buying into her mother's dreams, Harriet followed her own path, which led her first to northern California in 1902 and a position on the *San Francisco Dramatic Review*. She also occasionally contributed features to the *San Francisco Chronicle*. She was one of the first journalists to use a typewriter and was fascinated by anything mechanical.

In 1903 Quimby moved to New York as drama critic for *Leslie's Illustrated Weekly*, moving quickly through the ranks to feature writer. Seeking a new story, she covered the Belmont Park aviation meet in 1910 and was thoroughly captivated by the fliers, especially John Moisant's winning race around the Statue of Liberty. Harriet asked Moisant to teach her to fly, which he agreed to do, but he was killed in an air crash shortly afterwards. The school that Moisant had intended to found on Long Island was begun without him, however, and Quimby was one of the first to enroll.

Aviation was new and exciting news. It was also an extremely dangerous avocation, resulting in one hundred deaths in 1911 alone. As a journalist Quimby was well aware of what a sensation it would cause if word leaked out that a woman was learning to pilot an aircraft; consequently, she kept her plans to herself until after she received her license, making two nearly perfect test flights to do so. Her talent was not a secret for long, however, for as she was taking off a few weeks later, one of the tires exploded on the runway, causing the plane to tilt and smash. Reporters scurried toward the wreckage, and one morning edition of a newspaper featured Quimby's photograph plastered across the page with the headline, "Dresden-China Aviatrix."

After designing a plum-colored satin flying suit with a hood that became her trademark, Harriet joined the Moisant International Aviators, an exhibition team. Her debut with the group was a moonlit flight over Staten Island for twenty thousand spectators, a feat for which she earned fifteen hundred dollars. While she was touring with the group in Mexico City they performed for the inauguration of that country's new president, and Quimby began thinking about crossing the English Channel, a little-attempted feat and not one previously done by a woman.

In 1912 she sailed to England, secured sponsorship from and a promised story in the London *Daily Mirror*, and then was off to France to borrow a plane from the manufacturer, Louis Bleriot. She had no experience with a compass, which was essentially her only navigation tool for the flight, but her friend, British aviator Gustav Hamel, offered a quick lesson. Then, because he was concerned for her safety and likely fearful that she or any woman was incapable of such a flight, he offered to dress in her plum-colored garb, cross the expanse himself, and exchange places with her in France. Quimby declined.

Weather delayed her takeoff for several days, but on April 16 Quimby soared into the air, reached an altitude of fifteen hundred feet in thirty seconds, and was immediately swallowed by a monster fog. With extra layers of clothing and a hot water bottle hanging around her waist to keep herself warm in the open cockpit, Quimby skirted the Channel at a mile a minute, clutching the compass between her knees. She realized that, without visual contact, she might miss her landing in Calais, France, and she dropped the tiny monoplane one thousand feet to escape the fog. Although she could not spot Calais, she did recognize the coast of France and, exhausted, she set the aircraft down on a beach at Hardelot. Shortly, people raced out to greet her. From the smattering of French she could comprehend, it sounded as if they were congratulating themselves for her landing on their beach.

Ironically and tragically, the oceanliner *Titanic* struck an iceberg and sank while Harriet was in England waiting for better weather; consequently, her landmark flight received only a smattering of attention, buried in the back pages of the world's press. Nonetheless, personally triumphant, she returned to the United States and to the flying circuit. She had used her prize money to purchase a new, all-white, seventy horsepower Bleriot monoplane, which she proudly brought to the Squantum airfield for the Harvard-Boston meet on the last day of June 1912. Although the plane was considered unstable with a passenger on board, a fact that had caused several fatalities, Harriet agreed to take air show manager William A.P. Willard up for a spin over Dorchester Bay and around the Boston Light. It was a twenty-minute flight.

Quimby circled the Light, flew back toward the shore and began the descent for landing. Without warning, the nose dipped perpendicular to the water and the machine rocketed downward. The crowd of 5,000 watched as William Willard's unseatbelted body flew out of the plane as if he had jumped, arcing up, then down, and falling past the plane. Quimby struggled to regain control, but seconds later she too came hurtling through the air. She and Willard hit the shallow water at approximately the same time, crushed to death on impact.

More than being the first American woman to pilot an aircraft, Quimby should be remembered for being a visionary. When others were walking on wings and taking short flights over fields to show off their skill, she saw aviation as more than a sport; she saw the potential for ferrying passengers, delivering parcels, and taking aerial photographs. In many ways she was years ahead of her time.

References and Suggested Reading

Brown, Sterling A., and Dorothy I. Zaykowski. *First Lady of the Air: The Harriet Quimby Story.* Tudor Publishers, 1999.

Harriet Quimby Annual Research Conference, Giacinta Bradley Koontz, Director. *aviatrix@earthlink.net*

Holden, Henry M. *Her Mentor Was an Albatross: The Autobiography of Harriet Quimby.* Black Hawk Publishing Company, 1993.

Wilcox, Shirley. "Aviatrix Harriet Quimby: She Showed the Way." *American History Illustrated* (November 1985): 22.

Sally Kristen Ride
(1951–   )

United States
Astronaut/Physicist

Courtesy of NASA

I n 1982 Sally Ride soared skyward from the launching pad of the Kennedy Space Center to become the first American woman in space. She served as flight engineer on the seventh voyage of the space shuttle *Challenger*, returned to orbit with the thirteenth launch, and served as a role model for thousands of young women.

Sally Kristen Ride was born in Encino, California, in 1951. Her father, Dale Burdell Ride, was a professor of political science and her mother, Carol Joyce, volunteered at a women's correctional institute. As a child Sally enjoyed peering through a telescope and surveying the night sky, but her real passion was athletics. A self-styled tomboy, she wanted to play professional football but turned instead to tennis. She joined the junior tennis circuit and was ranked eighteenth nationally.

In 1968 Ride enrolled at Swarthmore College in Pennsylvania and planned to major in physics but dropped out after one year to continue touring with tennis teams. She returned to school in 1970 at Stanford University, acquiring both a bachelor of arts and a bachelor of science in 1973 as the result of a double major in physics and English literature. In 1978 she was awarded a doctorate in astrophysics.

While she was working on the final requirements for her degree, Ride applied to the National Aeronautics and Space Administration (NASA) as one of the wave of women applicants to answer the call for a new breed of astronaut. From thousands of applications she was selected as one of two hundred eight finalists, and in 1977 she was admitted to shuttle mission specialist training. During months of instruction Sally learned to fly a jet (a requirement for all astronauts), received her pilot's license, and spent hundreds of hours in a simulator, a device that replicates the antigravity of space travel. Her first assignment was to work with a team designing a remote mechanical manipulator arm that was used to deploy and retrieve satellites in space.

From 1981 to 1982 Sally Ride served as "capcom," the person who relays instructions from the flight director on the ground to the shuttle crew members. At the end of that tenure, she was selected to be the first American woman to go into space. After rehearsing for as many as fifty-six hours straight, Ride was buckled in and waiting the countdown of the seventh voyage of the shuttle *Challenger*. The only necessary accommodation for the lone woman among a crew of four men was the addition of a curtain across the lavatory entrance. The *Challenger* revolved in space for six days, during which the astronauts deployed several satellites. To round out a stellar year, after returning to earth, Ride married fellow astronaut Steven Alan Hawley.

In 1984 the pioneering woman was once again aboard the *Challenger* for her second mission and flight thirteen. During that orbit the team deployed the Earth Radiation Budget Satellite. Following that success, Ride served as acting head of the NASA Office of Exploration, a liaison position between the space administration and private defense contractors or aerospace companies seeking to purchase room for experimental projects on board the shuttle.

When the *Challenger* broke apart on takeoff in 1986, killing all those on board including her fellow astronauts Judith Resnick and teacher Christa McAuliffe, Ride reluctantly joined the presidential commission investigating the accident. Citing a momentary lack of trust in the program, she resigned from NASA the following year.

After leaving the space program Sally Ride joined the faculty of the University of California as a professor of physics, wrote children's books, and directed the California Space Institute. In 1999 she added Internet entrepreneur to her resume as a member of the board of directors of space.com. The realization of a childhood dream, Sally Ride once again sailed into the air in March 2000 on the maiden voyage of Goodyear's newest blimp.

References and Suggested Reading

"Dobbs adds Sally Ride to space.com." *Content Factory*, 30 June 1999, 100.

Eberhart, Jonathan. "Ride Report: The Going, Not the Goal." *Science News*, 22 August 1987, 132: 117–118.

"Ready When You Are." *Time*, 27 October 1986, 128: 49–50.

"Ride Is First U.S. Woman to Shuttle into Space." *Instructor and Teacher* (August 1983) 93: 86–87.

Vradenburg, Sarah. "Former Astronaut Flies Maiden Voyage of Goodyear's Newest Blimp." *Knight Ridder/Tribune Business News*, 21 March 2000, 1.

Freya Stark
(1893–1993)

England
Middle Eastern Explorer

As an Arabist, Freya Stark did more than any other adventurer to raise awareness of the peoples of the Middle East. For one hundred years, she approached all of life with an open mind, shrewd observation, original thought, and receptivity, particularly to foreign cultures.

Freya Stark, though British, was born in Paris, France, in 1893. Her father, Robert, a brewer by trade, had married his cousin, Flora. Travel began early for Freya as the family circuited through England and Italy, eventually settling in London when she was only one. Her parents had very different dispositions and eventually separated. Divorce, however, was out of the question. After the separation Freya and her sister Vera moved with their mother to Italy. The young woman remained in contact with her father, from whom she learned toughness and self-reliance, and adopted the role of protector toward her mother.

After securing a home for the girls in Asolo, Flora Stark invested the balance of her funds in a factory owned by an Italian count and friend, Mario di Roascio, and spent most of her time at the business. The girls occasionally visited the factory, but when Freya was thirteen, disaster struck. A steel shaft from one of the machines caught her hair, pulling her off the ground, tearing her scalp and mangling one of her ears. Despite extensive surgery, she was scarred for life and always wore a hat to hide the disfigurement.

As a young woman Freya was an avid reader, and her favorite work was a tattered copy of *The Arabian Nights* she was given as a child. Even then, the pull of the East was strong. She was an avid reader and spoke several languages, including fluent Arabic in which she was self-taught.

When she turned seventeen, the count asked for her hand but, having never cared for the man, she emphatically turned him down. He married her sister and Freya enrolled at Bedford College for Women in England. One of her professors, W. P. Ker, became her mentor, encouraged her writing, and offered her her first taste of mountain climbing on an outing in the Alps.

At the onset of World War I Freya dropped out of school and enlisted as a nurse at a clinic in Bologna. She met and became engaged to Guido Ruata, a bacteriologist, but he abandoned her after she contracted a mild case of typhoid. She was transferred to England, where she worked as a censor and volunteered in an ambulance unit before returning to Italy. Poverty spread across Europe after the war and Italy was no exception. A classic survivor, Freya earned her living by gambling and smuggling art across borders.

She enrolled in the London School of Oriental Studies in 1926. That training served as the launch for decades of travel, beginning with her first trip to Lebanon and Damascus. In 1928 she visited the Jebel Druze, leaders of the Druze Rebellion, in the Syrian Desert south of Damascus, even though the area was under martial law at the time. Her report of the rebellion earned her first credit as a writer, a piece in *Cornhill Magazine*.

Moving from there to Baghdad, Freya studied Persian and moved into a section of the city considered by fellow Europeans as most unseemly because it was a hodgepodge of races and crime-ridden. She was surrounded by a secular mix of Arabs, Kurds, Assyrians, Bedouins, and Shiites. The Bedouins robbed visitors when they could, people shunned soap because they thought it unhealthy, women were cloaked in black from head to foot, and Freya, in her flowery dresses and beach hats, could not have been happier. When she accepted an invitation and visited a sheikh in the desert, that was the last straw and her British acquaintances, most of whom were condescending to the Iraqis, excluded her from their society.

Traveling by donkey and accompanied by Bedouin guides, Stark sought out the castle of Alamut in the Elburz Mountains in 1930. The castle had once been home to the famed secret Assassins, vengeful murderers drugged on hashish. The local people thought she was a religious pilgrim and allowed her to wander wherever she chose. From there she crossed the ten-thousand-foot Chala Pass, weaving her way through flowering thorns, and followed the Alamut River through Iran, mapping the region as she went. In the wild, remote area of Lamiasar, she discovered the third Assassin castle. The approach to the castle was too steep for her slippery shoes, so she removed them and scrambled up the hill in her stocking feet. Despite bouts of malaria and dysentery, she eventually found her way back to Baghdad, becoming for a time the editor of the *Baghdad Times*.

Back in Italy, where she always returned, Freya was awarded the Gold Medal of the Royal Geographic Society and the Burton Medal of the Royal Asiatic Society. She went on lecture tours and published *The Valley of the Assassins*. By 1934 she was more than ready to venture out again.

Hiring local guides with six donkeys and bringing along a few live chickens to eat en route, Stark set out to explore the walled cities of Wadi Hadhramaut in Saudi Arabia. She made it to the first and oldest, Masna'a, before contracting measles. She recovered, then relapsed, and was forced to convalesce in a local harem. Eventually, she had to be airlifted out by a Royal Air Force bomber.

In 1937 she returned to Saudi Arabia as part of a three-woman expedition with Gertrude Thompson, an archaeologist, and Elinor Gardiner, a geologist. The professionals were unaccustomed to people looking over their shoulders while they worked and they were exceptionally rude to the local population. Freya left them, traveling into the desert on her own excursion by camel. For her the journey was always more important than reaching a destination. The purpose of travel was discovering how humanity interacts and in exploring the cultural variances that make one place different from another. She published two books about this revelatory expedition: *A Winter in Arabia*, which expressed open hostility toward Gertrude Thompson and science in general, and *The Southern Gates of Arabia*, her best writing, which recounted the failure of the expedition but, in the process, served as a cultural record of a people. In this latter work she lauded the advantages of being a woman in Muslim society.

For the next few months she traveled in Europe, but feeling the growing sense of unease, Stark wrote to the Foreign Office to offer her services in case of war. When World War II erupted, she was posted to Aden as an Arabist for the Ministry of Information. Stewart Perowne, the chief of information at that site, became her friend, and the two spent a great deal of time together. In 1940 Freya was transferred to Yemen and then to Cairo to counter growing Fascist influence there. She launched the Brotherhood of Freedom, an anti-Fascist group. In the beginning there were two hundred members, one year later there were one thousand, and by 1942 the group numbered in excess of sixteen thousand members. Freya Stark was respected by generals, courted by the socially elite, and admired by young men. One of her proudest accomplishments was learning to drive, although she did so badly. She drove alone through Palestine and Syria and into Baghdad, staying on the road for the most part, to establish another branch of the Brotherhood in Iraq.

In 1943 Stark took her campaign to the United States, sailing on board the *Aquitania* as the only woman among five thousand troops. Her message of the plight and basic goodness of the Iraqi peoples was less well received in the United States than in other locales due to a traditional Zionist sympathy and support for the people of Israel.

When the war ended, Freya returned once again to Italy, restored the family home at Asolo, and worked for the Ministry of Information as a press attaché. Her old friend, Stewart Perowne, then the Oriental counselor at the British Embassy in Baghdad, visited over the summer of 1947. When he discovered he was being transferred to the West Indies, he sent Stark a telegram proposing marriage. She accepted, joined him in Barbados, but left after two months. Years of independence had curtailed her ability to settle down. In an attempt to win her back, Perowne purchased a Vespa motorcycle and toured with her through Libya and on to Paris in 1950. The reconciliation failed, and they were separated in 1952.

Freya was ready for something new. She wanted to view "layer upon layer of time" and toured fifty-five sites in Ionia and West Turkey that were connected to the classic civilizations of Greece and Rome. She followed the path of Alexander the Great and sought the Roman frontiers in Asia.

In 1961 she flew to the Far East, visiting Peking, and seven years later made a trek through Afghanistan and into Soviet Central Asia by Land Rover. She received the title of Dame, the equivalent of knighthood, in 1972.

Unwilling to surrender to old age, Stark accepted a different role at age eighty-three. She became a television star as the British Broadcasting Company (BBC) filmed her on a barge floating down the Euphrates and, at eighty-seven years of age, seated on a pony in the Himalayas. From there she made side trips to Java, Sumatra, and Bali.

In 1985 she was given the keys to the city of Asolo, Italy, where she died at the age of one hundred. A prolific writer, Stark had many titles in her canon. Although some of the earlier hardbacks are out of print, Modern Library released a paperback series of reprints in 2001.

References and Suggested Reading

Geniesse, Jane Fletcher. *Passionate Nomad: The Life of Freya Stark*. New York: Random House, 1999.
Geographical Magazine (obituary) (June 1993) 65: 5.
Ruthven, Malise. *Traveller Through Time: A Photographic Journey with Freya Stark*. New York: Viking Press, 1986.
Stark, Freya. *The Journey's Echo*. London: John Murray, 1963.

Junko Istibashi Tabei
(1939–   )

Japan
Mountaineer/Environmentalist

A lthough it is intrinsic to Japanese culture not to call attention to oneself, particularly if one is a woman, Junko Tabei became the first of four women to reach the summit of Mount Everest, the highest peak in the world, a point from which she was seen by the whole world. Since that ascent, she has trudged up the face of a mountain on every continent, and her goal is to climb the highest mountain in every country on Earth.

Junko Istibashi Tabei was born in Miharumachi, Japan, in 1939, one of seven children. Fortunately, Miharumachi was not an area decimated by military bombing, and although money was scarce, there was always enough food for the family. Nonetheless, Junko was a frail child and prone to illness. When she was ten, however, her teacher took the class on a field trip to Mount Nasu and encouraged the children to scale the six-thousand-foot peak. Junko made it to the top and, enriched by the clear, icy air, knew she had found her place.

In 1962 Tabei received a degree in English literature from Showa Women's University and took a teaching post. She continued to climb, defeating all the summits in Japan, including Mount Fuji, the highest. Seeking camaraderie, she joined mountaineering clubs, but many male members refused to climb with her. In 1966 she married famed climber Masanobu Tabei, despite the fact that her parents disapproved of the match because he was not a college graduate.

Discouraged by the lack of companions among the men, Junko formed the Joshi-Tohan (Women's Mountaineering) Club, the first of its type in Japan. She took a second job as editor of the *Journal of Physical Society* of Japan to fund expeditions. The first trek by the group was a successful ascent of Annapurna III in 1970, and Tabei surrendered the more traditional role of Asian women to be forever known as the "crazy mountain woman." She had earned the title.

In 1975 four Japanese members of the Joshi-Tohan set out to climb Mount Everest, the highest mountain in the world at 29,028 feet. Located in the Himalayas between Nepal and Tibet, Everest has always been the pinnacle, the virtually unattainable goal, of every mountaineer's dreams. Since mountain climbing became a sport, only a handful of people have attempted the ascent and even fewer have stood at the top.

By May 4 the women had struggled up the peak to a little over twenty-one thousand feet and set up camp for the night. During the night, Tabei was startled awake by a rumbling that sounded like thunder but then grew deafening. Although she had never seen one, she knew the warning immediately. An avalanche was moving down the face of the mountain.

The rolling slush slammed into the tent, burying the climbers under snow and ice and mashing everything together. Tabei noted that she was trapped under the other women who were sharing her tent before she lost consciousness.

When she came to, she was relieved first to know she was not dead and second to find she was free of the wake left by the avalanche. The Sherpas, porters from the Khumbu region of Nepal, had dragged the women from the snow by their ankles. All were alive. Though bruised and cut and with a wrenched back, Junko had not come this far to claim defeat. Crawling at times, she clawed ever upward, and twelve days later she became the first woman to set foot on the top of Mount Everest.

On their return the women were hailed as national celebrities, given television miniseries, and offered a sequence of personal appearances. Graciously, Tabei accepted the acclaim, but the fame made her uncomfortable. She vowed never again to seek corporate sponsorship, since it was her funding group that was driving the promotional tours. Mountain climbing, she felt, should be a solitary experience.

From 1980 to 1992 Junko Tabei became the first person of either gender to surmount peaks on the seven continents, including Mount McKinley in North America, Mount Kilimanjaro in Africa, Vinson Massif in Antarctica, Aconcagua in South America, Mount Elbrus in Russian Europe, Mount Kosciusko in Australia, and Carstensz in Asia. Her ambition was to climb the highest mountain in every country, and by 1992 Tabei had crested sixty-nine of the world's major mountains, including five different peaks in five different countries in one year.

She is an environmentalist and cleans the mountains as she goes. As director of the Himalayan Adventure Trust, a preservation society founded to care for Everest's environment, she was responsible for installing incinerators on the peak to dispose of climber's debris. She has become a role model for the youth in Japan, a position she takes very seriously.

References and Suggested Reading

"Hall of Fame Nominees." WomenSports (October 1980): 32.

Horn, Robert. "No Mountain Too High for Her." Sports Illustrated, 29 April 1996, 84: 5B–7B.

Uglow, Jennifer S. The International Dictionary of Women's Biography. New York: Continuum Press, 1982.

Alexandrine Petronella "Alexine" Tinne (1835–1869)

The Netherlands
Middle Eastern Explorer

Courtesy of the Library of Congress

Alexandrine Tinne spent most of her short adult life traveling in the Middle East. Although she did not always have a concrete plan and did not always succeed when she did have a plan, she heightened public awareness about the existence of slavery and added to the storehouse of geographic knowledge about remote regions.

She was born Alexandrine Petronella Tinne, shortened to Alexine, in 1835 at The Hague in the Netherlands. Her father, Philip, was an English merchant who imported sugar from the West Indies, and her mother, Henrietta van Capellen, was descended from a Dutch naval family. When Alexine was nine years old, her father died and she became one of the richest heiresses in the country. Her urge to travel began early, while taking short trips with her mother on ponies in Scandanavia and in horse carts in the Pyrenees mountains. As a young woman she studied Arabic, botany, and photography and was an accomplished pianist.

When she was in her twenties, Tinne, her mother, and her aunt, Adriana "Addy" van Capellen, traveled to the Middle East. They spent their winters in Egypt and their summers in Palestine, journeying out of both locations to explore the surrounding country. They toured the lands of the Bible, crossing the Sinai Desert by camel to view the Red Sea and sojourning in the ancient Syrian city of Palmyra founded by King Solomon.

It was the Nile River, the longest in the world, that fascinated Alexine. The Nile is created by the joining of two rivers, the White Nile and the Blue Nile, so labeled by the color of their waters. The White Nile weaves through Uganda and into the Sudan, merging with the Blue Nile at Khartoum in the Ethopian highlands. With no real plan of how to accomplish her goal, Tinne resolved to seek the undiscovered source of the northward flowing White Nile.

Her extravagantly outfitted expedition, including her mother and aunt, hordes of servants, supplies, one hundred camels, and her pet dogs, traversed the Nubian Desert to the city of Khartoum. There they continued by river, ferried upstream with all their regalia on a dahabiyah, a large sailing vessel with cabins and galleys used by merchants, government officials, and wealthy travelers. The vessel used for the Tinne expedition was as large as a modern cruise ship, and often the enormous craft had to be pulled through narrower passages by two hundred men. At one point they were forced to leave the waterway to venture inland, taking a caravan to Abu Hamed. Since it was their custom to travel in luxury and not to forego the rudiments of civilization, they hired six guides, thirty camel drivers, over one hundred camels, and assorted horses and donkeys for the eighteen-day junket.

Stopping to rest in Jebel Dinka, Alexine was overwhelmed by the plight of the people and appalled by the open trading in slaves. She purchased a herd of oxen to feed thousands of the starving natives and rescued one family from slavery by purchasing them. Malaria and black water fever were rampant in the city, and soon Tinne became ill. After five days of high fever and delirium, she canceled the expedition and returned to Cairo. The botanical collection she had gathered on the adventure was donated to the Imperial Herbarium of the Court of Vienna.

When she recovered from her illness, Tinne changed her travel plans to the Bahr el Ghazal River, a tributary of the Nile. She loaded camels with provisions for a six-month excursion, contracted five hundred porters, and hired seventy soldiers for protection. The expedition was barely underway when the monsoon season struck, burying the party in rivulets of mud hidden under inches of water. Other travelers in the region had turned back before the deluge, and the Tinne camp was cut off. The conditions were too soggy to tramp out and too unbearable to stay put. Eventually, food supplies were depleted, and the porters began to fight among themselves over what remained. In the midst of the chaos Henrietta Tinne contracted black water fever and died. Alexine was devastated, for not only had she had an extremely close relationship with her mother, she felt responsible for prodding Henrietta into the unknown. Guilt-ridden and having spent thousands of dollars, the young woman plunged into a deep depression. However, her Aunt Addy, who had stayed behind in Cairo, grew concerned for their welfare and commissioned a search party. Two months after Alexine was rescued, her aunt died.

Tinne spent the next eighteen months wandering about Cairo in mourning and dressed as an Arab. When the city became too hot in the summer of 1866, she purchased a yacht and sailed the Mediterranean. The variety of races and nationalities among her retinue of servants and the hangers-on collected during her travels caused quite a stir among the local population as her yacht boarded. After only a short voyage she found life on the sea rather dull and opted for a new journey.

Traveling to North Africa, Tinne determined to study the little-visited Tuareg people of the Sahara. She was warned that the people might not be receptive to outside visitors, but the information did little to discourage her. What did discourage her, however, were some of the entourage she had created. After crossing the Atlas Mountains, she became so irritated with what she perceived as disagreeable people that she turned the entire group around and marched them back to the point of origin.

She lightened her entourage and increased her load of supplies, including specially designed metal tanks for carrying large amounts of water. After obtaining a guide who could furnish introductions to the Tuarag people, she set out again. She reached the Murzug, currently Libya, at last, the first white woman to travel into that uncharted region. The people were as exotic as she expected; women and men alike wore black veils with eye slits and colored robes and rode camels decked out in multi-hued fabric and streamers. They seemed to find her fascinating as well—a rich and unmarried woman traveling alone was considered an oddity and too much responsibility. Rumors of her being a witch who could turn her favorite dog into a man circulated among the encampment.

One morning a likely prearranged fight broke out among the camel drivers. One of the Dutch men traveling with Tinne attempted to intercede and was decapitated for his efforts. Alexine emerged from her tent, raising her hand to demand silence, only to have it sliced off by one of the Tuareg. As the blood spurted from her wound, she was struck on the back of her head with a saber. She fell to the ground and lay there for sometime before dying. Conjecture, supported by confirmation from those involved, attributed the incident to greed. The Tuarags believed the water tanks were filled with treasures that they wanted for themselves. Her effects were looted and her body left unburied to desiccate and blow away with the sands.

When her will was read, her loyal employees were well compensated. She left her remaining funds to pension those who had served her and those she had set free.

References and Suggested Reading

Adelman, Joseph. *Famous Women*. New York: Ellis Lonow Company, 1926.

Oliver, Caroline. *Western Women in Colonial Africa*. Westport, CT: Greenwood Press, 1982.

Fanny Bullock Workman
(1859–1925)

United States
Mountaineer

Courtesy of the Library of Congress

Oने of the most scandalous of the Victorian women travelers, Fanny Bullock Workman explored most of Europe and the Far East, primarily by bicycle and dressed in sensible clothing. She and her husband penned nine travel books that for decades served as guides for future adventurers.

Fanny Bullock Workman was born in 1859 in Worcester, Massachusetts, the daughter of the former governor of the state, Alexander Hamilton Bullock, and Eliza Bullock, a wealthy socialite. She was educated in New England, Paris, and Dresden and married William Hunter Workman, a physician, in 1881. The couple had one daughter, Rachel, who grew up largely in boarding schools, and a son who died in infancy. Dr. Workman suffered from poor health and in an effort to heal himself, the Workmans relocated in Europe, settling first in Germany.

The move did improve his health, and between 1895 and 1899 the couple undertook a series of walking and cycling tours that led them across Europe, into Algeria, over the Atlas Mountains, and to the outskirts of the Sahara, not a jaunt for the faint of heart or the physically unfit. Never traveling unprepared, Fanny carried a whip to discourage stray dogs from nipping at their feet as the bicycles rolled past and a revolver in case of confrontations with people. They tried to stay in small inns along the way, but when those were unavailable, the couple took whatever accommodations were provided, occasionally sleeping in the back of a bar. The first of the travel books, *Algerian Memories* (1895), was a result of this trip. Although the photographs, the work of Fanny, were exceptionally good, the writing was somewhat pedantic, and the couple persisted in addressing themselves in the third person, which led to some awkward passages.

Their next outing in 1897 was a voyage to the Far East, visiting Ceylon, Java, Sumatra, Burma, and India. They bicycled fourteen thousand miles across India over a three-year period, often having to ford rivers or drag their wheels out of deep sand. Overall, Fanny Workman found the scenery dull and was disgusted by the poverty. The Workmans never lost their upper-class condescension and had little compassion for the plight of less fortunate peoples or for their native guides. Their expeditions would likely have gone more smoothly had they shown more patience and empathy toward those in their employ.

Although the flatter portion of the country may have bored the Workmans, the couple was thrilled when they reached the foothills of the great mountains. Switching from being a cyclist and explorer to being a mountaineer, Fanny Workman organized an expedition of which she, as always, was completely in charge and towed her husband in her wake. Between 1898 and 1912 they visited the Karakoram Mountain range eight times, exploring glaciers and surveying and naming numerous peaks, despite the fact that some were already named. In Pakistan one of those mountains, at over nineteen thousand feet, was given the title of Mount Bullock Workman.

Workman set an altitude record for women with an ascent of the twenty-one-thousand-foot Mount Koser Gunge in 1899 and then broke it on the loftier Pinnacle Peak in the Nun Kun range in 1902. Her photograph was taken on the snowy crest with her ice axe in her hand. She survived one near disaster when she stepped back just in time to keep from following her lead porter into a crevasse. Fortunately, she was not tied to the customary rope that joins mountain climbers together, however, the porter fell to his death. Although she could survive near-death incidents and physical deficiencies ranging from headaches to breathing problems, Fanny was troubled by competition and criticism. Often mismeasuring their conquests and discovering the already discovered, the Workmans became the frequent target of negative commentary. Those inaccuracies, coupled with her compulsion to be the record holder among those of her gender, led Workman to challenge claims by other climbers, and she willingly paid the expenses to double check the altitude of other climbers' feats, including Annie Smith Peck's record-breaking ascents in South America.

After returning to Europe she was a favorite on the lecture circuit, once giving thirty presentations in twenty-seven days. Despite her hatred of "sexist" scientists, she became the first woman to address the Royal Geographic Association since Isabella Bishop. The Workmans' next travel plans were delayed by the outbreak of World War I in 1914 and further, in 1917, when Fanny became seriously ill. The illness persisted for over eight years until her death in 1925. She left the bulk of her estate to Radcliffe, Wellesley, Smith, and Bryn Mawr colleges, from which the latter developed the Fanny Bullock Workman Traveling Fellowship.

References and Suggested Reading

Adelman, Joseph. *Famous Women*. New York: Ellis Lonow Company, 1926.

Middleton, Dorothy. *Victorian Lady Travellers*. New York: E.P. Dutton and Company, 1965.

Miller, Luree. *On Top of the World: Five Women Explorers in Tibet*. Frome, England: Paddington Press, 1976.

Appendix I: Vignettes of Other Women

Mary Bailey

(1890–1960)

England

Aviator

Pioneering British aviator, Lady Mary Bailey, the daughter of Lord Rossmore, earned her pilot's license in 1927. She was the first woman to fly across the Irish Sea.

In 1911 she married South African billionaire Abe Bailey with whom she would have five children. At the age of thirty-eight she made an epic solo flight round-trip from England to South Africa, across the Sudan to Tanganyika, and back over the Belgian Congo and the Sahara. She referred to the flight as a gesture of female independence and a statement of faith in light aircraft. Bailey continued to participate in international competitions and was awarded the Britannia Trophy in 1930.

Winifred Blackman

(1872–1950)

England

Anthropologist/Photographer

Winifred Blackman spent fifteen years traveling in Egypt, collecting folklore from ancient storytellers, and supplying modern medicine to heal the sick. She observed magicians who employed healing charms to cure particular maladies and questioned whether or not they could benefit pharmaceutical drug companies. Borrowing various specimens, Blackman delivered them to the Wellcome Historic Medical Museum in London, where the charms were analyzed and found to be effective. In addition, she collected over one hundred and fifty tattoo designs, some of which could be traced to 2000 B.C., which were worn as cures for ailments.

Anne Isabella Noel Blunt

(1837–1917)

British

Arabian Explorer

The granddaughter of Lord Byron, the English poet, Lady Anne Blunt was the first English woman to travel on and describe the Arabian peninsula. Although she had an erratic education, she learned to speak Arabic and trudged through Turkey, Algiers, and Egypt. In 1877 she conducted a desert expedition from Aleppo to Baghdad, covering thousands of miles, navigating down the Euphrates, and migrating with the Anezeh people. She and her husband, poet and diplomat Wilfred Scawen Blunt, bought an estate in Egypt in 1881, where they bred Arabian horses.

Diane Doran

(1955–)

United States

Primatologist

How does one replace a legend? Even more foreboding, how does one replace a legend who has become a martyr? That was the task that awaited Diane Doran when she was selected to replace slain animal activist Dian Fossey, working with the mountain gorillas of Rwanda.

Diane Doran was born in Utica, New York, in 1956, the middle child of five. Her father, a pneumatic tool foundry worker, and her mother, a public health consultant, were often dismayed by their daughter's rejection of traditional employment and her search for occupational fulfillment. Diane, on the other hand, could not comprehend why anyone who was unhappy would remain at a job just for money. In an attempt to appease her parents, she enrolled in a nursing program but decided early on that medicine was not her life's work. After changing course and subsequently graduating from Utica College in 1968 with a bachelor's degree in biology, Doran studied French, and despite her parents' consternation, she joined the Peace Corps. She was assigned to Zaire for two years as a high school science teacher. While in Africa, Diane developed malaria and a bout of parasitic infections but she came to love the country, the wildness of nature, and the free-roaming animal life. After talking with students who were conducting research on chimps, she realized that was what she wanted to do, and Africa was where she wanted to be.

Once her stint in the Peace Corps came to an end, she returned to the United States and enrolled in the State University of New York at Stony Brook, seeking a doctorate in anatomy. Her dissertation topic took her back to Zaire and the Ivory Coast to study pygmy and common chimpanzees. As she was awaiting approval of her dissertation, she spotted an advertisement for employment with the Digit Fund, the organization founded by Dian Fossey to oversee the Karisoke Research Center and the mountain gorillas. In essence, the group was seeking the right person to follow in Fossey's footsteps. Doran applied.

Before she had the opportunity to second-guess her choice, she was climbing 10,000 feet up Mount Visoke, a dormant volcano in northwest Rwanda. Breaking into a clearing in the mist of the rain forest, Doran viewed the habitat where primatological icon Fossey had cared for and defended her charges and the site where she was buried. The momentary chill that washed over the young woman disappeared with her first glimpse of the giant apes. She was immediately fascinated as she watched their mannerisms, so closely aligned with human behavior.

To distance herself from her predecessor and carve her own niche in history, Doran avoids physical contact with the gorillas, while befriending people involved in the project and in the community. Each day she selects one of the animals to observe, drawing relationships between their behavior and their surroundings. Thanks to Fossey's pioneering efforts, the government has set strict penalties for poaching, thus making daily life less threatening for Doran. Eventually, through the incorporation of Rwandan students, she hopes the project will be sustainable without outside intervention. In the meantime she enjoys an office that stretches to the horizon and work she considers meaningful.

Gertrude Caroline Ederle

(1906–   )

United States

Adventurer, swimmer

At nineteen years of age, Gertrude Ederle was the first woman to swim the English Channel, a feat which she completed two hours faster than any man who had spanned the distance before her. Periodically munching on chocolate, chicken legs and sugar cubes, she made the record-breaking crossing in August of 1926, taking her from Cap Gris-Nez in France to Dover in 14 hours and 39 minutes. Although the expanse gained her world fame, she was likely more interested in her father's promise of a small roadster if she succeeded.

The daughter of German immigrant New Yorkers and a child prodigy, Ederle broke the 880-yard freestyle record when she was only twelve, the youngest age at which any person had broken a world's records. She was a member of the New York Women's Swimming Association and won a gold and two bronze medals in the only five events open to women in the 1924 Olympics.

After her Channel crossing, Ederle participated in a vaudeville act, demonstrating swimming styles in a large tank of water. Deafness and a back injury ended her championship career in the water but opened new opportunity as a teacher of swimming to deaf children in New York City. More than that, however, Ederle aided in changing the prevalent perceptions of female athletes and inspired others to enter the field.

Mina A. Ellis

(1870–1956)

Canada

Explorer

Mina Ellis was born in Bewdley, Ontario, and graduated from the Brooklyn, New York, Training School for Nurses. For a time she served as superintendent of the Virginia Hospital in Richmond, Virginia. In 1901 she married Leonidas Hubbard, a journalist and explorer, who died two years later while exploring Labrador. Resolving to complete her husband's work, Mina organized an expedition in 1905 and crossed the northeastern part of the Labrador Peninsula. She became the first white person to cross the Great Divide between the Naskaupi and George rivers. On her return she gave an account to the American Geographical Association and published *A Woman's Way through Unknown Labrador* (1908).

Joan Rosita Forbes

(1893–1967)

England

Explorer

Joan Forbes was born in Lincolnshire and privately educated, and during her early years she became obsessed with maps. At the age of seventeen she married Colonel Ronald Forbes and traveled through India, China, and Australia. When they divorced, she trekked alone across Africa. She halted her travels to drive an ambulance during World War I. After the war she journeyed through the Far East and settled in Paris as a journalist. She was commissioned to write on the French colonialism in North Africa and criticized for her commitment to Arab nationalism. While conducting her research, she visited the remote Moslem Senussi sect and explored western Arabia and Morocco. Forbes penned five popular books reflecting her interest in politics and social conditions.

Sophia Heath

(1896–1936)

United States

Aviator

In 1919 the International Commission for Air Navigation banned women from commercial navigation. Sophia Heath overcame that restriction by qualifying on all medical and aptitude tests, including navigation, meteorology, engine-fitting, rigging, and theory of flight. Consequently, she became the first woman of all time to be employed as an airline pilot. Flying for the Royal Dutch Airlines, her first concern was improving air safety and reliability.

Exploring other interests, Heath founded the Women's Amateur Athletic Association in 1922. Additionally, she became a forceful advocate for the right of women to participate in the Olympics and addressed the International Olympic Committee (IOC) in Prague on overturning the 1926 ban on women competing in the games. In 1928 women were allowed to participate in the event.

Heath was the first woman to fly solo from South Africa to England, establishing a record for taking off and landing at fifty different airfields in a single day with only six refuelings.

Jill Heinerth

United States

Oceanographer

Jill Heinerth is an underwater cave explorer who believes exploration is more of a technological puzzle than an act of great heroism or athleticism. Based on her previous experience diving in Mexico and the Yucatan Peninsula, Heinerth was invited to join the United States Deep Caving Team Wakulla 2 Project in North Florida. Over one hundred and fifty international volunteers assisted with the project, which tested the Cis-Lunar MK-5P Rebreather, a closed-circuit, mixed-gas, electronically controlled underwater breathing device. As the only woman on the team, Heinerth set a new woman's world record for deep cave penetration, a total of nine and one-half hours underwater.

Jeanne Holm

(1921–)

United States

Aviator

American Air Force Officer, Jeanne Holm was born in Portland, Oregon. She joined the Women's Army Auxiliary Corps in 1942 and was commissioned as a second lieutenant the following year. By the end of World War II, Holm was promoted to captain and put in charge of a women's training regiment. She retired from the army shortly after the war but reenlisted in the Air Force.

From 1965 to 1972 Jeanne Holm served as Director of Women in the Air Force, fighting for changes in career opportunities, assignments, and the abolishment of discriminatory rules. She was an adviser to President Gerald R. Ford from 1976 to 1977. In 1973 Holm was promoted to major general, the highest rank ever held by a woman in all branches of the American armed forces. She was a strong supporter of women's rights, a member of the National Women's Political Caucus, and a founder of Women in Government.

Kara Hultgreen

(1965–1994)

United States

Aviator

An aerospace engineer, Kara Hultgreen was among the first women pilots to qualify to fly jets in combat and the first allowed to do so. When she crashed into the Pacific during a routine training exercise in October 1994, critics used her as a scapegoat to undermine the administration's decision to put women into combat. One conservative radio talk show host even claimed that women were better suited to serve drinks on board aircraft than they were to pilot them.

In an effort to vindicate Hultgreen and to save the program, the United States Navy conducted a salvage expedition to lift the plane from the bottom of the ocean. The investigation concluded that the F-14 Tomcat's engine had failed and that the accident could not be attributed to pilot error. Upon her death Hultgreen received military honors; she had paved the way for future women in combat.

Dora Keen

(1871–?)

United States

Alaskan Explorer

Dora Keen was born in Philadelphia and graduated from Bryn Mawr in 1896. After eight treks up the Alps, she made the first ascent in 1912 of Mount Blackburn in Alaska, a subarctic peak measuring over sixteen thousand feet. She trekked three hundred miles on foot and by boat over the Alaskan wilderness to the Yukon River, becoming the first woman to cross Skolai Pass. In 1914, in the company of three men explorers, Keen observed various Alaskan glaciers. She was admitted as a fellow in the Royal Geographical Society in London.

Claude Kogan

(1919–1959)

France

Mountaineer

Claude Kogan lived in Nice, France, and ran a swimwear factory. She began climbing in the Ardennes and the Alps and then made the first ascent of Mount Sakantay, almost twenty thousand feet, in the Peruvian Andes in 1952. From there Kogan tackled the Himalayas, cresting Nun in the Punjab and in 1954 Cho Oyo, nearly twenty-five thousand feet, the highest point for a European woman. As an honorary member of the Ladies' Alpine Club, she resolved to lead the Expedition Feminine au Nepal, on an international all-woman climb of Cho Oyo in 1959. She and three others were lost in an avalanche near Base Camp IV.

Elizabeth Hawkins-Whitshed Leblond

(1861–1934)

Irish

Mountaineer

Elizabeth Leblond tramped up Mont Blanc and the Grand Jorasses in 1882 and bicycled across Italy. She traveled in China, Russia, and Korea before settling in St. Moritz, Switzerland, where she learned to skate and toboggan. While in Switzerland, she helped design the Cresta Run for Olympic bobsledding.

She was the first woman to lead otherwise guideless ascents of the Piz Sella, Piz Zugo, and Disgrazia mountains in Italy. In 1900 Leblond and Lady Evelyn McDonnel made the first women's "rope" climb on Piz Palu. She always wore a skirt over pants but removed the skirt when climbing became difficult. In addition, she had a lady's maid accompany her as far as possible. Elizabeth Leblond was the first president of the New Ladies Alpine Club formed in 1907 and an authority on snow photography, publishing a textbook on the topic in 1895.

Jerri Nielsen

(1952?–   )

United States

Antarctic Explorer

At forty-six years of age, Dr. Jerri Nielsen, an emergency room doctor, went to "winter" in the wastelands of the South Pole, where it is dark for six months each year and the average temperature is 100 degrees below zero. She was the only medical doctor on staff to care for forty-one scientists and support staff.

During her stay, she discovered a lump in her breast and diagnosed it as cancerous by performing a biopsy on herself with ice as her only anesthetic. Aircraft could not land at that time of the year, thus the cancer-fighting drugs had to be parachuted onto the ice. Nielsen administered her own chemotherapy, while continuing to provide medical services for the other members of the expedition. Her experiences are recorded in *Ice Bound* (2001), written with Maryanne Vollers.

Edith "Jackie" Ronne

(1919?–   )

United States

Antarctic Explorer

Some explorers have peaks or roads named in their honor but Jackie Ronne is the only one who can claim an ice shelf. She was one of two women who were the first to spend the winter in Antarctica in 1946. Accompanying her husband, Norwegian explorer Finn Ronne, Jackie made her first excursion to the frozen terrain on a wooden ship. The Ronne expedition mapped the last unknown shoreline between Coats Land and Palmer Land. The area, which was named for Jackie Ronne, is a body of floating ice, more than five hundred feet thick and extending inland for more than five hundred twenty miles.

After navigating the roughest seas in the world, the ship rammed through pack ice that was three to seven feet thick. The couple established the first American base in the Antarctic and spent the winter in a twelve-foot-square home. Jackie sent weather reports back to Washington, wrote newspaper articles, and kept a detailed journey.

In 1971 she was flown to the South Pole for the sixtieth anniversary of its discovery by Roald Amundsen, another Norwegian, and returned to visit her original base with her daughter in 1995.

Sheila Christine Scott

(1927–1988)

England

Aviator

Sheila Scott made the longest solo flight around the world, covering thirty-one thousand miles. She also piloted the first light aircraft solo over the North Pole.

Scott was born in Worcester, England, and worked as a nurse and an actor in bit parts and repertory companies. Scott began flying in 1959 and won her first races in an ancient Royal Air Force bi-plane. By 1971 she had set over one hundred world records. She completed several round-the-world flights and became the first pilot to solo a light aircraft from equator to equator in 1971. During that circuit, the National Aeronautics and Space Administration (NASA) monitored her mental and physical reactions and measured air pollution along her route. She was the founder and first governor of the British section of the Ninety-Nines and initiated the British Balloon and Airships Club.

Gertrude Emerson Sen

(?–1982)

United States

Asia Explorer

In 1910 Gertrude Sen taught English in Japan and returned to the United States to edit *Asia* magazine. Ten years later she was commissioned to head an expedition around the world. In the Philippines, she flew with a stunt pilot and explored a five-mile cave, swinging from ledge to ledge to an underground lake and back up a ninety-foot rope.

Gertrude moved to an uncharted village in northeastern India where she had a house built for her. She remained there, devoting herself to improving conditions for the villagers and shunning the outside interference of foreigners.

Miriam O'Brien Underhill

(1900–?)

United States

Mountaineer

Born in New England, Miriam Underhill began serious climbing in 1924. She conquered the Torre Grand Dolomites in 1927, pioneering a style of climbing that became known as the Via Miriam, and completed the first complete crossing of Aiguille du Diable. In 1930 she skied down Mont Rosa and for a time was known as the greatest American climber. In 1932 she led the first women-only ascent of the Matterhorn.

Mary Vaux Walcott

(1860–1940)

United States

Mountaineer

Mary Vaux Walcott was born in 1860 in Philadelphia, into a family of Quakers who taught her to appreciate equality, travel, and nature. From her mother, Sarah, the young girl learned botany and painting, both of which she pursued on family treks to Canada and across the western United States.

Between 1887 and 1900 Walcott staked claim to several records as a woman mountaineer. She studied and photographed glaciers in the Selkirk Mountains in British Columbia, attacked Mount Abbot with the first expedition in 1897, and was the first woman to climb Mount Stephen in the Rocky Mountains.

Walcott was awarded honorary membership in the Alpine Club of Canada for her photographic survey that recorded changes in glaciers, a pioneering effort that took an entire day to produce only twelve photos. In 1905 those records were published in *The Glaciers of the Canadian Rockies and Selkirks*, which she composed with her brother, George.

With her friend Mary Schaffer she became the first woman to explore the Deutschmann Cave in British Columbia. Throughout each of her excursions, she painted wild flowers, eventually amassing over four hundred canvasses, which she donated to the Smithsonian Institute. While working with the Smithsonian, Mary met and married Dr. Charles Walcott, a paleontologist, in 1914.

After Walcott's death in 1927 Mary was commissioned by President Calvin Coolidge to study the living conditions on American Indian reservations. She visited more than one hundred reservations over six years and covered more than five thousand miles on horseback. Her discoveries of the deplorable conditions among those peoples incited her activism, and for the next decade she fought to improve life for Native Americans. She died in 1940 of a heart attack.

Lucy Walker

(1836–1916)

England

Mountaineer

The daughter and sister of famous Alpinists, Lucy Walker began climbing at age twenty-two. She participated in ninety-eight expeditions in twenty-two years, including being the first woman, in 1871, to climb the Matterhorn. Rather stockily built, Walker climbed in a white print dress, munched sponge cake, and gulped champagne as she trudged the incline. She became the second president of the Ladies Alpine Club at age seventy-six.

REFERENCES

Adelman, Joseph. *Famous Women*. New York: Ellis Lonow Company, 1926.

"Diving the Dream." *http://www.divegirl.com/walkulla2.html*

Fussman, Cal. "A Long Way from Home: Neither Dian Fossey's Brutal Death nor Her Mother's Fears Could Stop Diane Doran from Pursuing Her Dream: To Work with the Mountain Gorillas of Rwanda." *Life* (February 1990) 13: 54–61.

Mason, Felicia. "Female Pilot Deserves Honor, Not Questions." *Knight-Ridder/Tribune News Service*, 11 November 1994, 111K6402.

Nielsen, Jerri with Maryanne Vollers. *Ice Bound: A Doctor's Incredible Battle for Survival at the South Pole*. New York: Talk Miramax Books/Hyperion, 2001.

Society of Woman Geographers Web site. *http://www.iswg.org/*

"Surviving Life at the South Pole." *http://www.msnbc.com/news*

Tasker, Georgia. "Jackie Among the Icebergs." *http://www.iswg.org/vignett.htm*

Uglow, Jennifer S. *The International Dictionary of Women's Biography*. New York: Continuum Press, 1982.

Appendix II: Women by Category

ACTIVIST

Florence Catherine Douglas Dixie

ANTHROPOLOGISTS/ARCHAEOLOGISTS

Ruth Fulton Benedict
Ernestine "Dee Dee" Green
Margaret Mead

AQUANAUT

Sylvia Earle Mead

ASTRONAUTS/COSMONAUTS

Eileen Marie Collins
Mae Carol Jemison
Sharon Christa Corrigan McAuliffe (honorary)
Valentina Tereshkova Nikolayev
Sally Kristen Ride

AVIATORS

Jacqueline Marie-Therese Suzanne Douet Auriol
Geraldine "Jerrie" Cobb
Jacqueline Cochran
Elizabeth "Bessie" Coleman
Amelia Earhart
Amy Johnson
Beryl Clutterbuck Markham
Ruth Nichols
Harriet Quimby

CONSERVATIONISTS/ECOLOGISTS/NATURALISTS

Joy Friederike Victoria Gessner Adamson
Elizabeth Cabot Cary Agassiz
Meta Ann "Annie" Doak Dillard
Anne LaBastille
Marianne North

EDUCATOR

Sharon Christa Corrigan McAuliffe

ENTOMOLOGIST

Lucy Evelyn Cheesman

ENVIRONMENTALISTS

Rachel Louise Carson
Ernestine "Dee Dee" Green
Junko Istibashi Tabei

EXPLORERS

Harriet Chalmers Adams (Africa)
Delia Denning Akeley (Africa)
Mary Lenore Jobe Akeley (Africa/Canada)
Ann Bancroft (Arctic/Antarctic)
Gertrude Margaret Lowthian Bell (Middle East)

Gertrude Benham (Africa/South America)
Isabella Lucy Bird Bishop (Middle East/United States)
Louise Arner Boyd (Arctic)
Alexandra David-Neel (Asia)
Beatrice Ethel Grimshaw (South Pacific)
Mary Henrietta Kingsley (Africa)
Monica Kristensen (Antarctic)
Marianne North (Asia/Africa/North America/South America)
Freya Stark (Middle East)
Alexandrine Petronella "Alexine" Tinne (Middle East)

HUMANITARIANS

Geraldyn "Jerrie" Cobb
Mary Henrietta Kingsley

ICHTHYOLOGIST

Eugenie Clark

IDITAROD CHAMPION

Susan Butcher

JOURNALISTS

Florence Catherine Douglas Dixie
Beatrice Ethel Grimshaw

MARATHON SWIMMER

Diana Sneed Nyad

MOUNTAINEERS

Mary Lenore Jobe Akeley
Gertrude Benham
Arlene Blum
Annie Smith Peck
Junko Istibashi Tabei
Fanny Bullock Workman

OCEANOGRAPHERS
Eugenie Clark
Sylvia Earle Mead

PHOTOGRAPHER
Margaret Bourke-White

PHYSICIAN
Mae Carol Jemison

PHYSICIST
Sally Kristen Ride

PRIMATOLOGISTS
Dian Fossey
Birute Marija Filomena Galdikis
Jane Goodall

SAILORS
Isabelle Autissier
Clare Mary Francis

SPY
Marguerite Elton Baker Harrison

Appendix III: Women by Nationality

AUSTRIA
Joy Friederike Victoria Gessner Adamson

CANADA
Birute Marija Filomena Galdikis

ENGLAND
Gertrude Margaret Lowthian Bell
Gertrude Benham
Lucy Evelyn Cheesman
Florence Catherine Douglas Dixie
Clare Mary Francis
Jane Goodall
Amy Johnson
Mary Henrietta Kingsley
Beryl Clutterbuck Markham
Marianne North
Freya Stark

IRELAND
Beatrice Ethel Grimshaw

FRANCE
Jacqueline Marie-Therese Suzanne Douet Auriol
Isabelle Autissier
Alexandra David-Neel

JAPAN
Junko Istibashi Tabei

THE NETHERLANDS
Alexandrine Petronella "Alexine" Tinne

NORWAY
Monica Kristensen

RUSSIA
Valentina Tereshkova Nikolayev

SCOTLAND
Isabella Lucy Bird Bishop

UNITED STATES
Harriet Chalmers Adams
Elizabeth Cabot Cary Agassiz
Delia Denning Akeley
Mary Lenore Jobe Akeley
Ann Fulton Bancroft
Ruth Benedict
Arlene Blum
Margaret Bourke-White
Louise Arner Boyd
Susan Butcher

Rachel Louise Carson

Eugenie Clark

Geraldyn "Jerrie" Cobb

Jacqueline Cochran

Elizabeth "Bessie" Coleman

Eileen Marie Collins

Meta Ann "Annie" Doak Dillard

Amelia Earhart

Dian Fossey

Ernestine "Dee Dee" Green

Marguerite Elton Baker Harrison

Mae Carol Jemison

Anne LaBastille

Sharon Christa Corrigan McAuliffe

Margaret Mead

Sylvia Earle Mead

Ruth Nichols

Diana Sneed Nyad

Annie Smith Peck

Harriet Quimby

Sally Ride

Fanny Bullock Workman

Selected Bibliography

Adams, William Henry Davenport. *Celebrated Women Travellers of the Nineteenth Century*. New York: Dutton, 1903.

Allen, A. *Travelling Ladies*. London: Jupiter, 1980.

Barr, P. *A Curious Life for a Lady: The Story of Isabella Bird, Traveller Extraordinary*. London: Penguin, 1986.

Birkett, Dea. *Spinsters Abroad: Victorian Lady Explorers*. Oxford, England: Basil Blackwell, 1989.

Blake, S.L. "A Woman's Trek: What Difference Does Gender Make?" *Women's Studies International Forum* (1990) 4: 347–355.

"Collins and Columbia Launch Chandra." *Sky and Telescope* (October 1999) 98: 16.

Early, Julie English. "Unescorted in Africa: Victorian Women Ethnographers Toiling in the Fields of Sensational Science." *Journal of American Culture* (Winter 1995) 18: 67–76.

"Flyers." *American Quarterly* (Fall, 1979) 31: 556–571.

"Going Where No Woman Has Gone Before." *Christian Science Monitor*, 19 July 1999, 1.

Hamalian, Leo, ed. *Ladies on the Loose: Women Travellers of the Eighteenth and Nineteenth Centuries*. New York: Dodd and Mead, 1981.

Kaye, Evelyn. *Amazing Traveler, Isabella Bird: The Biography of a Victorian Adventurer*. Boulder, CO: Blue Penguin Publications, 1994.

Livermore, Beth. "Their Crystal World." *Women's Sports and Fitness* (November-December 1997) 19: 31–33.

Moorehead, Caroline. *Freya Stark*. London: Viking, 1985.

Morrell, Virginia. "Amelia Earhart." *National Geographic* (January 1998) 193: 112–136.

Pearce, R. D. *Mary Kingsley: Light at the Heart of Darkness*. Oxford: Kensal, 1990.

Scott, Denham. "Where Are They Now?" *Journal of the American Aviation Historic Society* (Fall 1968) 13: 3.

Unsuitable for Ladies: An Anthology of Women Travellers. Selected by Jane Robinson. Oxford: Oxford University Press, 1994.

Index

About the Author

JOYCE DUNCAN is on the faculty at East Tennessee State University where she teaches English and Service-Learning. She is the Managing Editor of the Sport Literature Association, editor of H-Arete listserv, and a freelance writer, editor, and photographer. Her previous publications include numerous contributions to reference books, including *Dictionary of World Biography, Masterplots II, Encyclopedia of Civil Rights in America, American National Biography, Great Events from History,* and *Encyclopedia of Popular Culture in the United States.*